MIND YOUR OWN MIND

Harnessing the Power of Your Thought for Success and Happiness,
Take Control of Your Thoughts and Transform Your Life

By

AMARNATH J. SHETTY

PREFACE

"Om Namo Bhagavathe Vasudevaya"

"Your mind is your greatest asset—nurture it, guard it, and let it flourish on its own terms."

This book, *Mind Your Own Mind,* is more than just words on paper; it is a journey of reflection, wisdom, and personal growth. As I pen down these thoughts, my heart is filled with gratitude and remembrance for three pillars of my life—my beloved mother, my father, and my wife—who are no longer with me but continue to guide my soul every day.

My mother, with her boundless love and unwavering faith in me, shaped my values and taught me the essence of resilience. My father, with his wisdom and strength, instilled in me the courage to face the world with dignity. And my wife—my backbone, my source of strength—stood beside me through every joy and sorrow, making life's burdens lighter and its joys richer.

Though they are physically absent, their presence is deeply etched in my heart and mind. This book is a tribute to them, a way to carry forward the lessons they imparted and the love they showered upon me. Through these pages, I hope to share insights that will help others navigate their own minds with clarity, purpose, and peace.

To my mother, father, and wife—I dedicate this book to you, with love and reverence

With profound reverence and deep gratitude, I bow to my Spiritual Masters, whose wisdom, guidance, and boundless compassion have shaped my journey. Their illuminating presence has been a beacon of light, moulding my thoughts, actions, and aspirations. Through their teachings, I have found clarity, purpose, and inner strength.

It is only by their grace that I am able to offer this humble work, a reflection of the wisdom imparted by them. May this book serve as a tribute to their divine influence and inspire seekers on the path of truth.

Ref.: SCWPF/Book-Mind/001/0425   Date: 03rd April, 2025

Foreword

"Mānaḥ yeva manushyāṇāṁ kāraṇam bandha-mokṣayōḥ" _ Mind alone is responsible for the bondage or liberation. To discipline the mind and channelize it's hidden potential to higher directions is the purpose of all spiritual practices.

In a world full of distractions, we often forget the most important journey begins within. "Mind Your Own Mind" is not just a call to introspection but a reminder that the mind is a powerful tool —when mastered, it leads to peace, clarity, and boundless freedom. This book authored by Shri Amarnath J Shetty Ji is an invitation to dive deeper into your true self, to break free from the noise, and to cultivate a mindset that serves the true purpose of existence. The wisdom shared through these pages here, is a humble offering, inspired by years of spiritual discipline, insight and practical experience. May this book guide the readers on the path of successful life, inner peace, freedom leading to Self-Realization.

Shri Amarnath J Shetty Ji has been serving Swami Chidananda World Peace Foundation as its General Secretary since 2022 and related to many selfless service organizations. I congratulate Mr. Shetty for his great work with his spiritual insight revealed in his first book "Mind your own mind" and I extend my heartfelt wishes for all success.

With prayer and blessings.

(Swami Brahmanishtananda)
Founder
Swami Chidananda World Peace Foundation

706, Horizon Homes Near Government Museum, Bejai (Dakshina Kannada), Mangalore, Karnataka (India) 5750
Email: chidanandawpf@gmail.com , www.chidanandawpf.org

ACKNOWLEDGMENTS

As I present *Mind Your Own Mind* to the world, I want to extend my deepest gratitude to those who have supported me throughout this journey. To the Webethon Team, whose dedication and encouragement have been invaluable—thank you for believing in this vision. To my family and friends, your unwavering support and love have been my greatest strength. This book is as much yours as it is mine.

With Warm Regards

Amarnath J Shetty

Table Of Contents

Chapter 1: Introduction

Tales Etched in Time

The sun shone brilliantly that day, casting a golden glow over the landscape as I stood by my house, taking in the mesmerizing sight before me. Verdant fields stretched endlessly, their emerald hues shimmering under the warm embrace of daylight. Towering trees swayed gently, whispering secrets to the breeze, while the air carried the sweet scent of earth and foliage. I felt as though I were living in paradise. Yet, in my innocence, I was too young to truly grasp the magnificence of nature's embrace.

My childhood unfolded in the heart of a bustling joint family, where laughter was abundant, mischief was endless, and time seemed to slip through our fingers like grains of sand. Life moved forward, and before I knew it, I had grown up, though those enchanting days remained etched in my soul.

Ours was no ordinary home—it was a grand palatial residence, built by my great-grandfather, a masterpiece of heritage and artistry. Nestled within a tranquil village, it stood as a silent sentinel to a century of history.

The house, with its towering arched doorways, intricate wooden ceilings, and sprawling courtyards, exuded an air of timeless elegance. Every carved pillar, every delicate floral motif, and every antique lamp held a story waiting to be told.

The façade itself was a tribute to an era when craftsmanship and grandeur walked hand in hand. The walls—strong, steadfast, and weathered by time—bore the fingerprints of generations who had lived, loved, and flourished within them. In the heart of the home lay a vast central courtyard, where golden beams of sunlight pirouetted upon the stone floors. It was the soul of the house, a place where elders exchanged tales over steaming cups of tea and where the unrestrained laughter of children once echoed.

The sprawling verandas, adorned with exquisitely carved pillars, provided the perfect retreat to soak in the cool evening breeze, evoking a time when life moved at a slower, more graceful rhythm.

This was not just a house—it was a living testament to heritage, a harmonious blend of nostalgia and pride. It was one of the most distinguished residences in our village, and within its walls, our family flourished. If my memory serves me right, there were more than twenty children among us, along with numerous other family members. Though the house had four distinct sections, for us children, there were no divisions. We were one—playing, fighting, and marching to school together, bound by an unspoken bond of unity.

Festivals, particularly Deepawali, were magical. The anticipation built up all year, as we diligently saved every penny to buy fireworks. When the grand day arrived, the house transformed into an ethereal vision—hundreds of diyas and oil lamps casting a warm, flickering glow, while bhajans and kirtans filled the air with devotion. Every festival, every ritual was a shared celebration, woven into the very fabric of our family's customs.

Growing up in a joint family shaped me in ways I would only come to appreciate later. It taught me the essence of love, patience, and the beauty of coexisting with diverse personalities. It was a world where affection reigned supreme, where bonds were unbreakable, and where the idea of 'mine' and 'yours' dissolved into 'ours.'

Until my fourth grade, this house was my entire universe. Then, my mother decided it was time for me to move to my grandmother's house in a nearby village for further studies. It was there that I entered a new world—a new school, a different environment, and unfamiliar faces. The school stood so close to our house that we could hear the ringing of the bell from our doorstep, summoning us to a world of learning and discipline.

I was a diligent student, and even now, I hold immense admiration for the school's vision, its rigorous curriculum, and the unwavering discipline it instilled in us. The structure of our education was unparalleled—firm yet nurturing, traditional yet ahead of its time. Beyond academics, we were immersed in an array of extracurricular activities: drama, skits, student-run courts and ministries, sports, and soulful bhajans and kirtans.

Who would believe that, 56 years ago, in the heart of a remote village, we played baseball with meticulously followed rules? Our school administrator was a visionary, a man who believed in molding well-rounded individuals, ensuring that we were exposed to a world beyond textbooks and lectures.

Even now, the walls of those classrooms remain vivid in my memory—not just for their bricks and mortar, but for the words of wisdom inscribed upon them. Beautiful phrases, written with care, adorned each classroom, etching themselves into our young minds. Some of those words still echo in my heart, guiding me, reminding me of the values instilled in those formative years.

And so, as time continues its relentless march forward, I find solace in the memories of those golden days—of a home filled with love, a school filled with wisdom, and a childhood that will forever remain a treasured chapter of my life.

One of the things that stayed with me from my school days were the beautiful phrases written on the walls of each classroom. These words, simple yet profound, were not just lessons in school but life's guiding principles. Even today, they echo in my heart, reminding me of the wisdom I was fortunate to receive in those formative years.

"Satyam Vada Dharmam Chara" – Speak the truth, practice righteousness.

"Vidya Dadati Vinayam" – Knowledge bestows humility.

"Atmanam Viddhi" – Know yourself.

"Satyameva Jayate" – Truth alone triumphs.

"Shikshaya Phalamadhigaccha" – Success in work brings success in life.

"Arogyam Mahabhagyam" – Health is a blessing.

Childhood Chronicles: Memories & Moments

The year was 1966. I was in seventh grade when something shifted within me—an intangible yet powerful change that altered the way I perceived the world. It was an age of innocent curiosity, yet I found myself grappling with questions far beyond my years. The news of suicides from nearby villages echoed through the town, whispered among elders, dismissed with sighs, and quickly brushed under the carpet. Each time I overheard such tragic tales, a strange unease settled in my mind.

"Why would someone choose to end their own life?"

It was a question that refused to fade. Whenever I attempted to ask my elders, they waved me off impatiently. "It's not your cup of tea. Don't poke your nose where it doesn't belong," they'd say. But the question had already taken root in my thoughts, growing wild with every passing day. At night, I lay awake, restless, staring at the ceiling, my young mind entangled in fears I didn't fully understand. Even in the classroom, the echoes of these unanswered questions followed me, leaving me distracted and detached.

One evening, a terrifying thought crept into my mind—one that I couldn't shake off. What if I were to end my life? The idea was neither sudden nor fleeting; it stayed, lingered, and eventually began to take shape as a plan. I was known as a bright student, active in extracurricular activities, well-liked by my teachers. No one could have imagined the turmoil brewing inside me. I wondered how my family would react, how they would grieve, whether they would finally understand the pain I had been carrying. The more I entertained these thoughts, the more determined I became to go through with it.

That Saturday, as I walked out of school, I felt a strange sense of finality. I had given away my hard-earned marks to my opponent in class, something I had never done before. "Why would you do that?" she asked, bewildered. I simply smiled and told her, "It's your day." No one knew that, in my mind, I had already decided it was my last.

I walked out of the school gates and stopped for a moment before the grand image of Mahatma Gandhi, painted on the school wall. Goodbye, I whispered, a lump rising in my throat. Tears welled up in my eyes as I thought of my teachers, my friends, my family. I reached home, hugged my grandmother a little tighter than usual—an embrace that confused my younger brother, who watched me with suspicion.

That evening, on our way to my father's house, I made a detour to a small grocery shop under the pretense of buying household essentials. I asked the shopkeeper for rat poison, weaving a convincing lie about a rodent infestation at home. He hesitated for a moment but eventually handed it over. I tucked the small packet into my pocket, feeling its weight against my leg, and walked away. My plan was in motion.

That night, surrounded by my family, the atmosphere was warm and lively. My mother served us dinner, my siblings chattered away, and my father made a passing remark about my unusual silence. My mother, ever intuitive, assured him I was probably just tired. If only she knew. I forced myself to eat, all the while envisioning the chaos that would follow the next morning.

Sunday arrived. The sun bathed the courtyard in golden light, laughter echoed from the veranda as the children played, and yet, I was lost in my own darkness. Clutching the poison in my pocket, I made my way to the bathroom—an open space behind our kitchen. My hands trembled as I opened the packet, my heartbeat a deafening roar in my ears. I closed my eyes and thought of my family one last time. And then, I swallowed.

The bitterness burned my throat, and within moments, my body rejected it. A violent wave of nausea overtook me, and I began to vomit uncontrollably. The retching sounds caught the attention of my father's sister, who rushed to my side. In my panic, I threw the remaining poison away before she could see. She helped me inside, her voice thick with concern as she called my mother. Someone rushed to bring herbal medicine, forcing it down my throat, triggering another round of vomiting. I was too weak to resist.

My mother stroked my forehead as I lay on the cot, dazed. They assumed it was food poisoning, never suspecting the truth. I survived that day—saved by fate, by the quick thinking of my aunt, by something greater than myself.

Lying there, exhausted but alive, a new realization dawned upon me. Maybe life had other plans for me. Maybe I was meant to live.

That secret, the darkest chapter of my childhood, remained buried in my heart for years. I never spoke of it—except to two close friends. But even today, when I look back, I remind myself of one unwavering truth:

"Everything passes at par, temporarily; truth alone remains permanently."

The Lingering Echoes of Childhood: When Emotions Turn into Despair

Childhood is often painted as a time of innocence, joy, and boundless curiosity. Yet, for many, it is also a period marked by deep emotional wounds—wounds that do not bleed but fester over time, growing into an unbearable weight. The emotions experienced in childhood, whether stemming from neglect, abuse, loneliness, or unfulfilled expectations, have a profound impact on the adult psyche. When these emotions remain unaddressed, they can culminate in a tragic attempt to end one's own life.

A Close Escape-My second incident

It was July 1967. I had just joined high school, a newly constructed institution still in its early stages. My father had wanted me to enroll in the one near our house, but my uncle insisted I join this new school, believing it would offer better opportunities. We were only the second batch of students to enter its classrooms, and though the school lacked finished infrastructure, it carried the promise of a fresh beginning.

Our classroom was adjacent to an unfinished building, where construction workers toiled each day, their hands shaping the walls that would one day stand tall. Among them was the contractor—a lively man who was not just in charge of the site but also worked as a plasterer. He was always smiling, always laughing, and always eager to share a moment of joy with us. Every afternoon, a group of us—about eight to ten students—would place our tiffin boxes in one of the unfinished rooms and gather there during recess. The contractor often joined us, sharing stories between bites of food, his presence warm and familiar.

That day, the sky was overcast, and a light drizzle coated the half-built walls with moisture. By mid-morning, the social studies class had begun, and as the lesson unfolded, our minds were already inching toward the lunch break at 12:30 p.m. The rhythmic sound of the teacher's voice filled the room, but at exactly 11:55 a.m., everything changed.

A deafening crash erupted through the air, shaking the ground beneath us. The walls trembled, the desks rattled, and for a brief second, silence gripped us—before chaos took over. Screams filled the corridor as students and teachers rushed outside, our hearts pounding in our chests.

What we saw sent a chill down our spines. The building under construction, the very place where we kept our tiffin boxes, had collapsed into a heap of broken bricks and dust. And buried beneath it was the contractor.

The sight was too much to comprehend. Just minutes ago, he had been there, his laughter echoing in the corridors, his presence as steady as the walls he built. Now, those very walls had betrayed him, swallowing him in an instant.

The teachers quickly took control, shielding us from the scene, ushering us away before we could witness the full horror of what had happened. Police arrived, surveying the wreckage and cordoning off the area. The headmaster, his face grim, announced that the school would remain closed for the day.

As I walked home, my legs felt heavier with every step. The contractor's face—his smile, his laughter—kept flashing before my eyes. Only forty minutes later, and that rubble could have been my grave. The thought sent shivers down my spine. Tears welled up in my eyes, and by the time I reached home, I could no longer hold them back.

Word of the incident spread like wildfire. There were no mobile phones or instant news updates in those days—only whispers passed from one anxious mouth to another. My parents, gripped by fear, did not know whether I was safe until someone finally brought them the news.

Even now, all these years later, my heart races when I think of that day. That was my second close brush with death in my childhood. The second time fate had spared me. And in that moment, I realized—life is uncertain, unpredictable, and fragile. But for some reason, my journey was meant to continue.

Perhaps, even then, the universe was shaping me for something more.

Chapter 2: The Foundation Of Self-Awareness

"One who sees inaction in action and action in inaction is intelligent among men, and he is in the transcendental position, although engaged in all sorts of activities."

— Bhagavad Gita 4.18

Self-awareness is nothing but the ability to recognize and understand one's emotions, thoughts, and behavioural patterns. In our day to day life we are not able to identify our thought process and emotions and which leads us to have a stressful life .Let us understand what is self Awareness

Understanding Self-Awareness

Self-awareness is the foundation of personal growth and emotional intelligence. It refers to the conscious knowledge of one's emotions, behaviour's, and thoughts. Being self-aware allows individuals to assess their strengths and weaknesses, recognize their values, and understand how their actions impact others. All the events you have experience in your life time from your childhood days up to this moment have been created by your thought patterns and the belief you held in the past . You are always thinking of the words and thoughts you used month ago. A year ago or more year ago or your childhood memories. These are all past memories and its all over and done . What is important is the present moment and be in the present moment and that create your future by forming the experience of tomorrow and years to come. One of the Book which I read On Spiritual Intelligence Authored by Danha Zohar and Co authored by Ian Marshell

There are seven Practical steps to better SQ (Spiritual Quotient) and self awareness

- Become aware of where I am now

- Fell strongly that I want to change

- Reflect on my own centre is and what are my deeper motivations

- Discover and dissolve obstacle

- Explore many possibilities to go forward

- Commit myself to a Path

- Remain aware there many Paths

The Importance of Self-Awareness

Developing self-awareness is crucial for personal and professional success. It helps in making informed decisions, managing stress, and improving relationships. A self-aware person is more adaptable to change and can handle challenges with a balanced mindset.

Every day we have many feelings. Sometimes we are happy. Sometimes we are sorrowful, sometimes angry irritated or afraid; and these feelings fill our mind and heart. One feeling last for a while and another comes, and another as if there is a stream of feelings for us to deal with , Practising meditation is to be aware of each feeling .

The Abhidharama writings on Buddhist psychology say that feelings are of three kinds; pleasant unpleasant and neutral. When we step on a thorn we have unpleasant feeling. When someone says something nice to us, "you are very smart" or "you are beautiful, we have a pleasant feeling. And there are neutral feelings such as when you sit there in a quiet place and feel either pleasant or unpleasant . A so-called neutral feeling can become very pleasant. If you sit beautifully and practice breathing and smiling. You can be very happy when you sit in the way, aware that you have feeling of wellbeing. That your eyes are capable of seeing. forms and colours , Isn't it wonderful

Depends upon our way of looking . We call seeing a neutral feeling. If someone has lost her sight would give anything to be able to see, and if suddenly she could, she would consider it a miraculous gift . we who have eyes sees many form of colours are often unhappy, If we want to practice , we can go out and look at leaves, Flowers, Children and Clouds and be Happy .

If you practice awareness you suddenly become very rich , very very happy. You need to help yourself to it. All of us have the capacity to transforming neutral feeling into pleasant feeling , very pleasant feeling that can last a long time. This is what we practice during sitting and walking meditation .

If you want your world at happy and peace , you need to practice this

When there is Righteouness in the Heart

There is Beauty in the Charecter

When there is Beauty in the Charecter

There is Harmomy in the Home

When there is Harmony in the Home

There is Order in the Nation

When there is order in the Nation

There is Peace in the World

Challenges in Becoming Self-Aware

Despite its benefits, achieving self-awareness can be challenging. Many people struggle with self-criticism or denial when confronting their weaknesses. In child hood if we did some mistake and hide with our parents and teachers, It will remain in your subconscious mind for ever unless its addressed properly. It is important to develop a balanced perspective by accepting both strengths and areas of improvement.

Conclusion

Self-awareness is a lifelong journey that leads to personal and professional growth. By continuously reflecting on our thoughts and actions, we can enhance our emotional intelligence, build stronger relationships, and lead a more happier in life

Some of the points which I would like to share here for the benefit of the readers , which I Learnt from my CBT Therapy Course(Cognitive Behavioural Therapy)

Mind is a rare Psychological state that a peson occupies in their day to day life . It is the Quiet optimal mode of acting or thinking, that is flexible , adaptive and Holistic

There are Three Spheres of Human Cognition

Emotional Mind. The wise Mind and Reasonable Mind

Emotional MIND

- Regressive – Moving backward or returning to an earlier state of mind, less advanced state.

- Unreasonable – Lacking logic, fairness, or rational justification.

- Discontented – Feeling dissatisfied or unhappy with a situation, some times in our family relationship as well

- Reactive – Responding to situations after they happen rather than proactively addressing them. Some times in life we are not able to address the situation properly ,then we regret later what went wrong .

THE WISE MIND

Balancing is the wise Mind

- Reflective – Engages in deep thought, analyzing past experiences for insight and learning.

- Philosophical – Explores fundamental truths and questions about existence, meaning, and knowledge.

- Contemplative – Spends time in thoughtful consideration, often seeking deeper understanding.

- Growth-Oriented – Focuses on self-improvement, learning, and evolving through experiences.

- Considerable – Worthy of attention, significant in impact or thought.

- Self-Awareness – Has a clear understanding of one's emotions, thoughts, and behaviors.

REASONABLE MIND

- Intellectual

An intellectual mind is highly focused on information, analyzing facts with precision and logic. However, this intense focus can sometimes lead to a sense of disconnection from emotions and intuition.

- Disconnected

A disconnected mind may feel detached from emotions or surroundings, prioritizing logic over feelings. This can lead to objective decision-making but may also create a sense of isolation.

- Information

An informative mind seeks and shares knowledge, valuing accuracy and clarity. It focuses on delivering facts and insights to enhance understanding.

- Focussed

A focused mind stays dedicated to the task at hand, minimizing distractions and maintaining clarity. This sharp concentration enhances efficiency and goal achievement.

1. Types of Self-Awareness

   o Internal Self-Awareness – Understanding your emotions, values, strengths, and weaknesses.

   o External Self-Awareness – Understanding how others perceive you.

Emotional regulation is the ability to manage and respond to emotions in a healthy and constructive manner. Strengthening this skill can lead to improved mental well-being, better decision-making, and healthier relationships.

Ways to Enhance Emotional Regulation:

Mindfulness and Self-Awareness – Practicing mindfulness helps individuals recognize and accept their emotions without being overwhelmed.

2. Cognitive Reframing – Changing the way one perceives a situation can help reduce negative emotional responses . Cognitive reframing is a mental strategy that involves shifting perspective on a situation to alter its emotional impact. By challenging negative or limiting thoughts and replacing them with more constructive interpretations, individuals can reduce stress, enhance resilience, and improve decision-making.

3. Deep Breathing and Relaxation Techniques – Exercises like deep breathing, meditation, and progressive muscle relaxation can calm the nervous system. That is where the Yoga and Spirituality play a big role in our day to day life . Deep breathing and relaxation techniques help calm the nervous system, reduce stress, and improve overall well-being. By focusing on slow, deep breaths, you can lower heart rate, ease tension, and enhance mental clarity. Practicing regularly promotes a sense of peace and mindfulness.

Healthy Expression of Emotions – Writing in a journal, talking to a trusted friend, or engaging in creative activities can help process emotions effectively. .Use "I" statements (e.g., "I feel hurt when..." instead of "You always..."). Speak calmly and respectfully, even when upset. Avoid suppressing or ignoring emotions, but also avoid acting impulsively. Take a pause before reacting when emotions are intense.

1. **Developing Problem-Solving Skills** – Addressing the root cause of distress and finding practical solutions can prevent emotional escalation.

When I was counselling one young boy who was around mid-twenties whom I happened to met him on face book and he wanted to join my online Yoga class. He was from U.S and when I met him first time for the initial introduction meeting, I could gather from his face and body language, either he may

be having drinkimg habit or may be some drug abusive case .
I thought of convincing him by providing his family history
and some CBT questionaries. Initially he was very much
reluctant to give me the feedback of his family history and
finally with rigorous fallow up he provided me the family
details He was not answering my questionaries , I said without
answering my questions we will not move further and he
submitted the questionaries but some of the answers were
vague., but its o,k for me and I could understand his feelings
and behavioural patterns.

He was from a very good family back ground and his
parents were divorced 5 years back . He joined my course and
I was just counselling him and not teaching any yogic Practices
Except Yoga Nidra and Meditation. He was with my session
for almost 2 months and I was taking the sessions weekly
twice. I could see his behavioural patterns are changing day by
day and he was responding very well. Some time later he was
absent for many sessions and not responding my message
either.. One day suddenly at night he called me and I was in
deep sleep and he said I am moving to some other town for my
job and I am not able to attend your session till I am settled
and he was in confused state of mind what to speak further . I
told him its o,k. and we can discuss this in day time. Next day
I got a message "Thank you Sir for your valuable Support and
you are a good trainer and what about my fees ?., I replied to
him its o,k and take care of yourself and your life on a serious
note and not to worry about the fees. I tried my best to solve
his problem and prayed for his better future and he never
turned back .

2. **Building Resilience** – Strengthening coping mechanisms through positive self-talk, gratitude, and self-care can enhance emotional stability . Practicing Self talk in fromt of the Mirror as soos as get up by feeding the positive affirmation to the mind .

The Mirror and the Monk story

In a quiet monastery on the edge of a vast forest, a young monk named Ravi struggled with frustration. He often found himself annoyed by others—one monk chewed too loudly, another walked too slowly, and yet another always interrupted conversations. No matter where he went, something irritated him.

One day, the wise old master noticed Ravi's troubled expression and asked, **"Why do you seem so restless, my child?"**

Ravi sighed. **"Master, I try to stay peaceful, but the habits of others disturb me. I don't understand why they can't change."**

The master smiled and handed Ravi a small, round mirror. **"Take this and walk around the monastery. Each time you feel annoyed, look at yourself in the mirror before speaking or reacting."**

Though confused, Ravi obeyed. At first, he saw only his frustration reflected back at him. But as the days passed, something changed—he noticed that his face twisted with irritation whenever he got annoyed. He realized that it wasn't just others' habits that were the problem—it was how he reacted to them.

One evening, Ravi returned to the master, bowing deeply. **"Master, I see now. The problem was never them. It was my own mind that needed to change."**

The master nodded. **"Self-awareness is the first step to peace, my child. When you understand yourself, the world around you begins to change as well."**

From that day forward, Ravi focused not on changing others, but on understanding himself. And as he did, the world seemed far less irritating than before.

Chapter 3: Unravelling Thought Patterns

"Until you make the unconscious conscious, it will direct your life and you will call it fate."

— Carl Jung

Unraveling Thought Patterns refers to the process of identifying, analyzing, and reshaping the way we think. Our thoughts influence our emotions, behaviors, and overall mental well-being. Sometimes, we develop negative or unhelpful thinking patterns that lead to stress, anxiety, or self-doubt. By recognizing these patterns, we can challenge irrational beliefs, reframe perspectives, and cultivate healthier mental habits. Techniques such as cognitive restructuring, mindfulness, and self-reflection help in breaking these cycles, allowing for clearer thinking and better decision-making. This process is essential for personal growth, emotional resilience, and improved mental health. On average, humans have around 60,000 to 80,000 thoughts per day. This means we generate about 2,500 to 3,300 thoughts per hour or roughly 40 to 55 thoughts per minute!

However, not all of these thoughts are new—many are repetitive or based on habits. Studies suggest that a large percentage (up to 80%) of our daily thoughts are negative or self-critical, and around 95% are the same thoughts we had the day before.

It's fascinating how our minds are constantly at work, even when we're not fully aware of it! Have you ever noticed yourself having the same thoughts repeatedly?

- **Explore the nature of thoughts and how they shape our reality.**

Our thoughts are the invisible architects of our reality. Every idea, perception, and belief we hold influences how we experience the world, interact with others, and shape our future. Let's explore the nature of thoughts and their profound impact on reality.

The Nature of Thoughts

Thoughts are mental constructs that arise from the brain's processing of information. They can be rational or irrational, conscious or subconscious, fleeting or persistent. Some key aspects of thoughts include:

- Cognitive Processing – Thoughts help us analyze situations, solve problems, and make decisions.

- Emotional Influence – Our thoughts are deeply tied to emotions, shaping our mood and overall well-being.

- Neuroplasticity – The brain has the ability to rewire itself based on repetitive thought patterns, meaning thoughts can literally change the brain's structure.

How Thoughts Shape Reality

1. Perception Filters Reality: Each person's reality is unique because thoughts act as filters. A positive thinker sees

opportunities in challenges, while a negative thinker may see obstacles everywhere.

2.   Self-Fulfilling Prophecies: What we believe about ourselves and the world often manifests in our lives. If we think we are capable, we take actions that lead to success; if we doubt ourselves, we hesitate and may fail.

3.   The Power of Focus: Where attention goes, energy flows. Focusing on negative experiences amplifies them, while focusing on gratitude and possibilities can create a more fulfilling reality.

4.   Thoughts and Vibrations: Some philosophies, such as the Law of Attraction, suggest that thoughts emit energy that attracts similar energies. While scientifically debated, there is evidence that mindset influences behavior, which in turn shapes outcomes.

5.   Subconscious Programming: Many of our deep-seated beliefs and habits come from repetitive thoughts. By reprogramming our subconscious with positive affirmations and visualization, we can alter our experiences.

Harnessing the Power of Thought

•   Mindfulness & Awareness – Observing thoughts without judgment helps us understand how they shape our reality.

•   Reframing Negativity – Consciously shifting negative thoughts to positive perspectives can change experiences.

- Visualization & Affirmations – Imagining desired outcomes and reinforcing them with affirmations can program the mind for success.

- Gratitude & Positivity – Regularly focusing on gratitude rewires the brain for happiness and resilience.

Final Thoughts

Thoughts are not just passive re**flections of reality; they actively create it. By becoming aware of our thought patterns and intentionally guiding them, we have the power to shape our lives in extraordinary ways.**

Negative thought patterns can be sneaky, but identifying and challenging them is key to improving mental well-being. Here are some effective strategies:

1. Identify Negative Thought Patterns

- **Keep a Thought Journal** – Write down negative thoughts when they arise to recognize patterns. When we are Doing Our spiritual Sadhana our guru had instructed us to wite 5 mistakes daily on our Sadhana Journal . Initially a thought came to my Mind what is the use of this writings daily but the importance I could understand during our review session . Weekly we had a sadhana sessions and we need to review our mistakes . The outcome is whenever you are doing some mistake repeatedly, its deep rooted in your subconscious mind . if we give the proper auto suggestions to the mind then it will erase gradually .

Example : Mr Amit had heavy workload in the office and returned home late in the night . He had not informed his wife that he would be late in returning and when his wife questions him about where he had been ? , He replied to her very rudely.

Personality Defects : Short tempered and arrogance

Auto suggeession: When I reach home late I get angry when my wife asks me where I had been ; I will realise that she is questioning for my own good , because she is concerned about me . Therefore I will politely reply that I was busy in the office due to heavy work load.

• **You are the Product of your thoughts and habits** – You are creating your life when you choose your thoughts and you choose your psychologhy And When you choose your Psychlogy you choose your Behaviour . And when you choose your Behaviour you choose the consequence of that behaviour which includes wealth or poverty . Bottomline is you are the creater of your wealth and you are the creator of your poverty . What kind of thought do you have .Your thoughts have the real power

They have the power over your life . they have the power over your abilities , what kind of choices have you made in your life ?,

You have been creating your life since lomg , long time ago. Even if you are not aware of it . By the choices you have made in the past you have created your life . You are where you are right now because of the choices you have made .

- Recognize Cognitive Distortions – Common ones include:

  - All-or-Nothing Thinking – Seeing things as either perfect or a total failure.

  - Overgeneralization – Assuming one bad event means everything will go wrong.

  - Mind Reading – Believing you know what others think (and assuming it's negative).

  - Catastrophizing – Expecting the worst-case scenario.

2. Challenge Negative Thoughts

- Ask for Evidence – Is there factual proof supporting the thought, or is it an assumption?

- Consider Alternative Explanations – What's another way to view the situation?

- Talk to Yourself Like a Friend – Would you say this to a loved one in the same situation?

- Test Your Thoughts – If you fear failure, take a small action to challenge that belief.

3. Replace with Positive and Balanced Thoughts

- Reframe the Thought – Instead of "I'll never succeed," say, "I may struggle, but I can improve."

- Use Affirmations – Positive self-statements like "I am capable" can shift your mindset.

- Practice Gratitude – Focusing on positives counterbalances negativity.

4. Develop Healthy Mental Habits

Mindfulness & Art of Breathing – Helps you observe thoughts without reacting to them.

Teach Children -The Art Of Long Breathing

An important part in building a child character is to teach him to concentrate. The Practice has to start from Child hood to get good result Later. Along with the practice of concentration, children will power also to be strengthened and increased. If at the Age of 7 every child is taught of three things –Control over Emotions, Concentration and Developing will Power – then parent would ever complain about their children's behaviour later . These three factors help to flourish the seeds of Good Samskaras, values in the child. A child is similar to a fertile land on which it is necessary to cultivate

Good values and virtues.

The Challenge is How to Instil such virtues in our child? The first solution to this challenge is the practice of Long Breathing. The child should be taught to breath Long, and he should practice it so frequently that eventually he would take 4 to 5 breaths in one minute. Even 5 to 10 minutes of such practice would bring noticeable changes in the child behaviour. He will be able to control his anger and keep away from intoxicants. All intoxicating things are generally taken in order to relieve oneself from tension. It makes you experience heavenly bliss for a moment. The natural Characteristics of a

Person who takes long breath is that he would be living in the present and would not entertain false happiness, Long breathing will give him everlasting Bliss, which Alcohol or Drug cannot Provide.

The Single solution to millions of bad habits is long breathing. The kids who have short tempered should be made to practice long breathing regularly. Their behaviour would improve definitely. Not only for kids this is infallible solution for every person. Whenever one angry, one should practice long breathing for 5 to 10 minutes; the anger would disappear automatically.

It is proven fact that when out breaths are short , the tendency to loose temper is more. Long breath nullify the feet of any negative proven emotion. One can never lose control if practicing long breathing. Relaxation is another way to relieve stress. One Practice Kayotsarga (Complete Relaxation body from Head to Toes), Shavasana and Yoga Nidra have obtained the formula of living without tension.

Long breathing and Kayotsarga are the infallible steps to control emotions and relieve tensions. These would instil good values in children. But these values will take shape only if the parents are aware about them.

Once a Judge asked a thief "Why do you to enter people's Homes? i warned you several times not to do so ". The thief replied, ' Sir I always remember your advice and try to follow it , but what can i do , whenever I see welcome written on the door I cannot stop myself and do the same mistake to land up here again .

We either do not understand the facts properly or try to avoid understanding them. How will a noble character will take shape i this case? It is necessary to know the truth and consider the importance of instilling good values in children and ourselves. If we teach our children to get control over their emotions and develop their concentration and will power , then we can truly help our children and shape their character better than anyone else.

What we need to learn society as a whole to see that children get literacy on how to control Emotion. anger and stress. These are all psychological problems, if we take care of this in childhood itself, they get consistent message on emotions and how to handle it in all parts of their lives. Children learn their lesson of their life. Even the parents have to be taught how to deal with the children regarding emotional literacy.

Cognitive Behavioral Therapy (CBT) Techniques – Professional guidance can help rewire thought patterns.

Cognitive Behavioral Therapy (CBT) provides valuable insights into Fixed Mindset vs. Growth Mindset, helping individuals shift toward more adaptive thinking patterns. Here are some key points:

Fixed Mindset (Limiting Beliefs)

- Belief: "My abilities are fixed; I can't improve."

- CBT Insight: This belief leads to avoidance, fear of failure, and low resilience.

- Example Thought: "I'm just not good at math, so there's no point in trying."

- CBT Strategy: Challenge the thought: "What evidence do I have that I can't improve? Have I tried different strategies?"

Growth Mindset (Adaptive Thinking)

- Belief: "Skills and intelligence can be developed with effort."

- CBT Insight: Encourages persistence, problem-solving, and emotional regulation.

- Example Thought: "I struggled before, but if I practice, I will get better."

- CBT Strategy: Use positive self-talk and reframe failure as a learning opportunity.

CBT Techniques for Shifting Mindsets

Cognitive Restructuring – Identify and challenge negative self-talk.

Behavioral Experiments – Test whether effort leads to improvement.

Self-Compassion & Gratitude – Recognize progress and small wins.

Journaling & Affirmations – Reinforce growth-oriented beliefs.

By applying CBT principles, you can shift from a Fixed Mindset to a Growth Mindset, leading to greater success, resilience, and well-being.

- **Surround Yourself with Positivity – Spend time with supportive people who uplift you.**

There is one saying, tell me who is your friend and then I will tell who you are? . You will become how the company you keep. Always keep a friend with whom you can share your feelings and thought openly .

Surrounding yourself with positivity means choosing to spend time with people who support, encourage, and inspire you. Positive relationships help boost your confidence, reduce stress, and promote a healthier mindset.

When you surround yourself with uplifting individuals, you're more likely to stay motivated, embrace challenges, and maintain a hopeful outlook on life.

Conversely, being around negativity can drain your energy and hinder personal growth. Choose to cultivate relationships that bring joy, encouragement, and positivity into your life.

Break the Cycle – Engage in activities that distract and uplift (exercise, hobbies, socializing).

Breaking the cycle of monotony, stress, or negative habits requires proactive efforts in key areas of life. Three essential components—socializing, exercise, and hobbies—play a crucial role in enhancing mental and physical well-being.

1. Socializing

Helps combat loneliness and fosters emotional support.

Engaging with friends, family, or community groups can provide motivation and a sense of belonging.

Networking and meeting new people can open doors to fresh opportunities and perspectives.

2. Exercise

Physical activity boosts endorphins, improving mood and reducing stress.

Regular workouts enhance energy levels, focus, and overall health.

Group exercises or sports can combine fitness with socializing, making it more enjoyable.

3. Hobbies

Pursuing interests like reading, painting, music, or gardening can provide a creative outlet.

Hobbies serve as a distraction from stress and negative thought patterns.They contribute to personal growth, skill development, and relaxation.

By integrating these elements into daily life, one can break unhealthy cycles and build a more fulfilling and balanced lifestyle.

The Echo Chamber

Aarav had always believed that the world worked in patterns—predictable, repetitive, and unchangeable. Every morning, he followed the same routine: coffee, newspaper, work, home, repeat. His mind was a fortress of familiar thoughts, reinforcing what he already believed to be true.

One day, a glitch in his predictable world forced him to pause. His favorite café was closed, forcing him to try a new one across the street. The barista, Maya, greeted him with a warm smile. As they chatted, she asked, *"Do you ever challenge your own thoughts?"*

Aarav chuckled. *"Why would I? I know what I believe."*

Maya leaned in and said, *"But have you ever questioned where those beliefs come from?"*

The question lingered in his mind. That evening, he caught himself observing his thoughts, something he had never done before. He realized how many of them weren't truly his—they were echoes of past experiences, societal norms, and unexamined fears.

Curious, he started journaling, questioning his automatic thoughts. The more he unraveled, the more he realized how much of his life was guided by unconscious assumptions. Slowly, his thought patterns shifted. He became more open, more curious, more aware.

Chapter 4: How to Cultivate Mindful Living

"Your own Self-Realization is the greatest service you can render the world."

- Sri Swami Ramana Maharshi

Mindful living is about being fully present in each moment, appreciating life as it unfolds. It involves awareness of thoughts, emotions, and surroundings without judgment. By practicing gratitude, deep breathing, and intentional actions, we cultivate inner peace. This way of living reduces stress, enhances well-being, and deepens our connection with ourselves and others

Cultivating mindful living involves being fully present and aware in each moment, without judgment.

Every human being on this planet wants to lead a healthy, happy and successful life. How to achieve and enjoy the life is a big question .Let us see what are the best possible ways to cultivate Mindfull living '

1. **Practice Meditation** – Set aside time for mindfulness meditation to enhance awareness and focus. I am into Yoga and Spirituality for the past Four decades , with my learning and practicing for the past four decades ,If you start practising I can assure you that you will be cultivating Mindfull living

Mindful living involves cultivating present-moment awareness, and meditation is a key practice to achieve this. Here are different types of meditation that support mindful living:

Mindfulness Meditation

Focuses on observing thoughts, emotions, and sensations without judgment.Often practiced with attention on the breath, bodily sensations, or sounds.Helps develop awareness and presence in daily life.

Focused Attention Meditation

Involves concentrating on a single object, such as the breath, a candle flame, or a mantra.Strengthens attention, reduces distractions, and improves concentration.

Loving-Kindness Meditation (Metta Meditation)

Cultivates feelings of compassion and love for oneself and others.Involves silently repeating phrases of goodwill, such as "May I be happy, may you be safe."Promotes emotional well-being and positive relationships.

Body Scan Meditation

Focuses on systematically scanning the body from head to toe. Helps release tension, increase body awareness, and reduce stress.

Transcendental Meditation (TM)

Uses a silent mantra repeated internally to promote relaxation. Aims to transcend ordinary thought and access a deep state of restful awareness .Meditation that Takes You Beyond All limits .

According to Maharshi Mahesh Yogi " Mankind was not Born to Suffer, Mankind was born to Enjoy Life. The Purpose of Life is to Expand Happiness. Human beings can get rid of their, suffering

Attain state of happiness and share it with others by practicing the techniques of Bhavteet Dhyana. Transcendental Meditation (TM).TM is withdrawal of consciousness and senses from the external object and concentration of the consciousness on the self .

Dhyan is Different From Upasana the method of worship Upasana depends on the religion , faith upheld by one , So there cas be as many Upasana methods of Worship .

Dhyan means concentration of mind on God or Self or the Supreme Principle or Even Shunyas . Nothingness in Budhism . almost similar techniques of Dhyan called Vipasana. Upasana on the Other hand , In conscious thought of Him . For example , Nam Jap , recitation of names of God is a form of Upasana ,

The Word Transcendental means going beyond the limits of human knowledge , reason , Reason . TM is a method of claiming the mind becoming relaxed by thinking deeply in silence repeating a syllable or series of word (Mantra) many times in a row.

In the preface of Maheshi Yogi Science of being and Art of Living , chlares F Lutes writes that the Term " Transcendental Meditation " though seems very complicated and difficult to understand simply means a scientific   method of " Communication With the Infinite " . Its a scientific because it is system and produces measurable and predictable results The Outcome of TM is realisation and fulfilment of the Art of realisation .

The chief purpose of this meditation technique is to put one in touch with his own essential self, the eternal being within by moving ones attention away from the suffering and stress .

One then becomes the Absolute Being, and experience which Maharshi calls God Consciousness.

The Practice does not require any prior understanding of any philosophical Theory All that is required of the Practitioner is to recite twice a day for about 15 – 20 minutes a day a string of words Ie Mantra , with closed eye . The Mantra is chosen by the trained teachers guru according to the need of the Practitioner, The TM is also called the Guru Centred Practice.

The Regular Practice of TM eliminates the negative feeling of Stress and fatigue and replaces with them the positive feeling of wellbeing. The change has been scientifically proven by many researcher's. TM is not a passive State, rather it is the state of restful alertness where the mind is awake but Quiet .

Zen Meditation (Zazen)

A traditional Buddhist practice involving sitting in a specific posture and observing thoughts.Encourages a deep awareness of the present moment without clinging to thoughts.

Zen meditation, or **Zazen**, is a form of meditation rooted in Zen Buddhism. It emphasizes seated meditation, mindfulness, and deep concentration. Unlike other meditation techniques that focus on visualization or mantras, Zazen typically involves observing thoughts without attachment, focusing on the breath, and cultivating awareness of the present moment.

How to Practice Zen Meditation (Zazen)

Find a Quiet Space – Choose a calm environment with minimal distractions.

Sit in the Right Posture – Traditionally, practitioners sit in the **lotus or half-lotus position** on a cushion (zafu) or a chair with an upright spine.

Hand Position (Mudra) – The **cosmic mudra** is common, where the hands rest in the lap, forming an oval shape with thumbs touching lightly.

1. **Focus on the Breath** – Pay attention to natural breathing, often by counting breaths or focusing on the sensation of air moving in and out of the nose.

2.   **Observe Thoughts Without Judgment** – Rather than suppressing thoughts, allow them to come and go without attachment.

3.   **Keep the Eyes Open or Half-Open** – Unlike some meditation styles, Zazen often involves maintaining a soft gaze downward to stay grounded.

4.   **Practice Regularly** – Even **10–20 minutes a day** can be beneficial, but many Zen practitioners engage in longer sessions.

Benefits of Zen Meditation

- **Improves Focus & Clarity** – Zazen enhances **mental discipline** and helps improve concentration.

- **Reduces Stress & Anxiety** – By fostering mindfulness, it helps calm the nervous system and **reduces overthinking**.

- **Promotes Emotional Balance** – Helps cultivate **inner peace, patience, and resilience** to life's challenges.

- **Enhances Self-Awareness** – Encourages deep introspection and awareness of one's thoughts and behaviors.

- **Supports Better Sleep** – A relaxed mind leads to **improved sleep quality** and reduced insomnia.

- **Encourages Presence & Mindfulness** – Practicing Zazen makes it easier to live in the **present moment** rather than dwelling on the past or future.

- **Strengthens Compassion & Empathy** – Helps cultivate a more **compassionate outlook** toward oneself and others.

Guided Meditation

Involves listening to a teacher or audio recording guiding the meditation process.Helps beginners by providing structured instructions.

Chakra Meditation

Focuses on energy centers (chakras) in the body to promote balance and healing. Uses visualization, breathwork, or sound (such as chanting).

Chakra meditation is a practice that focuses on aligning and balancing the body's seven main energy centers (chakras) to promote overall well-being. Each chakra is associated with a specific location, color, and aspect of life. By meditating on each chakra, you can clear blockages, enhance energy flow, and improve mental, emotional, and physical health.

The Seven Chakras & Meditation Focus:

1. **Root Chakra (Muladhara)** – Red

   o Location: Base of the spine

   o Focus: Grounding, stability, security

o   Meditation: Visualize a red light at the base of your spine, feel grounded, and repeat the mantra **"LAM."**

2.   **Sacral Chakra (Svadhishthana)** – Orange

o   Location: Lower abdomen

o   Focus: Creativity, pleasure, emotions

o   Meditation: Imagine an orange glow in your lower belly, embrace creativity, and chant **"VAM."**

3.   **Solar Plexus Chakra (Manipura)** – Yellow

o   Location: Upper abdomen

o   Focus: Confidence, personal power, willpower

o   Meditation: Envision a bright yellow sun at your stomach, feel empowered, and repeat **"RAM."**

4.   **Heart Chakra (Anahata)** – Green

o   Location: Center of the chest

o   Focus: Love, compassion, connection

o   Meditation: Picture a green light expanding from your heart, radiate love, and chant **"YAM."**

5.   **Throat Chakra (Vishuddha)** – Blue

o   Location: Throat

o   Focus: Communication, self-expression, truth

o   Meditation: Visualize a blue light at your throat, speak your truth, and chant **"HAM."**

6.   **Third Eye Chakra (Ajna)** – Indigo

o   Location: Forehead, between the eyebrows

o   Focus: Intuition, wisdom, inner vision

o   Meditation: Imagine an indigo light at your third eye, trust your intuition, and repeat **"OM."**

7.   **Crown Chakra (Sahasrara)** – Violet or White

o   Location: Top of the head

o   Focus: Spiritual connection, enlightenment

o   Meditation: See a violet or white light at the top of your head, feel connected to the universe, and meditate in silence or with the mantra **"AUM."**

How to Practice Chakra Meditation:

Find a quiet space and sit comfortably.

Close your eyes and take deep breaths.

Focus on each chakra, starting from the root and moving up.

Visualize the corresponding color and energy center.

Use mantras or affirmations to enhance energy flow.

Spend a few minutes on each chakra or focus on one that needs balance.

End the meditation with gratitude and grounding

Yoga Nidra (Yogic Sleep)

A deeply relaxing meditation done while lying down in Shavasana Pose .Guides the practitioner through different stages of consciousness, leading to profound rest.

In My yoga session I teach and guide yoga nidra with full body awareness fully relaxation mode and give some positive affirmations which takes around 12 to 15 minutes

Yoga Nidra, also known as **Yogic Sleep**, is a powerful relaxation and meditation practice that guides you into a state between wakefulness and sleep. It promotes deep rest, healing, and inner awareness.

Key Aspects of Yoga Nidra

- **Systematic Relaxation** – Involves guided instructions to relax different parts of the body.

- **State of Consciousness** – You remain aware while entering deep relaxation.

- **Stress Relief & Healing** – Reduces anxiety, improves sleep, and enhances mental clarity.

- **Accessible to All** – No physical movement required; practiced lying down.

How It Works

1.   **Set an Intention** – A Sankalpa (resolve) is mentally affirmed.

2.   **Body Scan** – Awareness moves systematically through the body.

3.   **Breath Awareness** – Deepens relaxation and focuses the mind.

4.   **Visualization** – Images or scenes may be guided to access the subconscious.

5.   **Return to Wakefulness** – You gently come back to normal awareness.

Yoga Nidra is often used for **deep relaxation, emotional healing, and even spiritual exploration**.

12. Sound Meditation

Uses sound, such as Tibetan singing bowls, gongs, or chanting, to induce relaxation and mindfulness .Helps calm the nervous system and deepen meditative states.

Breathe Consciously

Pay attention to your breath, using it as an anchor to stay present.

Breath Consciously: A Deeper Insight

Breathing is one of the most fundamental aspects of life, yet most people take it for granted. "Breath Consciously" refers to the practice of bringing awareness to your breath, regulating it with intention, and using it as a tool to enhance physical, mental, and emotional well-being.

1. The Science Behind Conscious Breathing

The idea that there are 72,000 nerves in the human body comes from ancient yogic and Ayurvedic traditions, particularly in relation to nadis—the energy channels in the body. In yoga and Ayurveda, it is believed that there are 72,000 nadis that carry prana (life energy) throughout the body, with three main ones:

Ida Nadi – Associated with the left side of the body, cooling energy, and the moon.

Pingala Nadi – Associated with the right side, heating energy, and the sun.

Sushumna Nadi – Runs through the spine and is linked to spiritual awakening.

However, from a scientific perspective, the human body has billions of nerves, forming the nervous system (central and peripheral). The brain alone has around 86 billion neurons! The nervous system is responsible for transmitting electrical and chemical signals to coordinate movement, sensation, and bodily functions.

Breathing is directly connected to the autonomic nervous system, which has two main branches:

- **Sympathetic Nervous System (Fight-or-Flight):** Rapid, shallow breathing triggers stress responses, increasing heart rate and cortisol levels.

Operates through the **vagus nerve** and releases **acetylcholine** as its main neurotransmitter.

The **sympathetic nervous system (SNS)** is part of the **autonomic nervous system (ANS)**, which controls involuntary body functions. The SNS is responsible for the **"fight or flight"** response, preparing the body for stressful or emergency situations.

Functions of the Sympathetic Nervous System:

1. **Increases Heart Rate** – Helps pump more blood to muscles.

2. **Dilates Pupils** – Improves vision in low light.

3. **Inhibits Digestion** – Redirects energy to essential organs.

4. **Relaxes Airways** – Increases oxygen intake.

5. **Stimulates the Release of Glucose** – Provides quick energy.

6. **Contracts Blood Vessels** – Raises blood pressure.

7. **Activates Sweat Glands** – Helps cool the body.

8. **Stimulates Adrenal Glands** – Releases adrenaline and noradrenaline.

Neurotransmitters Involved:

• **Norepinephrine (Noradrenaline)** – The primary neurotransmitter that activates SNS responses.

• **Epinephrine (Adrenaline)** – Released from the adrenal glands to enhance SNS effects.

Comparison with the Parasympathetic Nervous System (PNS):

• The **SNS** activates the body for action (**fight or flight**).

• The **PNS** calms the body down after stress (**rest and digest**).

• **Parasympathetic Nervous System (Rest-and-Digest):** Deep, slow breathing activates relaxation responses, lowering stress and promoting healing.

• The **parasympathetic nervous system (PNS)** is a division of the autonomic nervous system responsible for **rest and digest** functions. It counterbalances the sympathetic nervous system, promoting relaxation, energy conservation, and digestion. The PNS lowers heart rate, enhances digestion, and stimulates activities like salivation and urination. It primarily operates through the **vagus nerve** and releases **acetylcholine** as its main neurotransmitter.

By consciously altering our breath, we can influence our nervous system, emotional state, and overall health.

2. Benefits of Conscious Breathing

- **Reduces Stress & Anxiety:** Slow, rhythmic breathing lowers cortisol and activates the vagus nerve.

- **Enhances Focus & Clarity:** Oxygenating the brain improves concentration and cognitive function.

- **Boosts Immune Function:** Proper breathing supports lymphatic drainage and detoxification.

- **Improves Sleep:** Deep breathing before bed calms the mind and prepares the body for restful sleep.

- **Balances Emotions:** Conscious breathwork can help regulate mood and increase emotional resilience.

- **Strengthens the Lungs & Heart:** Proper breathing improves oxygen flow, strengthening the cardiovascular and respiratory systems.

3. Types of Conscious Breathing Practices

A. Diaphragmatic (Belly) Breathing

- Breathe deeply into the belly instead of shallow chest breathing.

- Inhale through the nose for 4 seconds, hold for 4 seconds, and exhale through the mouth for 6-8 seconds.

- Helps with relaxation, digestion, and mental clarity.

B. Box Breathing (Square Breathing)

•   Inhale for 4 seconds → Hold for 4 seconds → Exhale for 4 seconds → Hold for 4 seconds.

•   Used by Navy SEALs to stay calm under pressure.

C. Alternate Nostril Breathing (Nadi Shodhana)

•   Balances energy and calms the mind.

•   Inhale through one nostril, close it, exhale through the other, and repeat.

D. 4-7-8 Breathing (Relaxation Method)

•   Inhale for 4 seconds, hold for 7, exhale for 8.

•   A powerful technique to reduce stress and induce sleep.

4. Integrating Conscious Breathing into Daily Life

•   **Morning:** Start your day with 5 minutes of deep breathing to energize your body.

•   **Work/Stressful Situations:** Practice box breathing to remain calm and focused.

•   **Exercise:** Sync breath with movement for improved endurance.

•   **Before Bed:** Do 4-7-8 breathing to promote deep sleep.

- **During Meditation:** Use breath as an anchor to stay present.

Conclusion

Breathing consciously is a simple yet powerful practice that can transform your health, mindset, and quality of life. By taking control of your breath, you take control of your emotions, thoughts, and overall well-being.

2. **Engage in Daily Activities Mindfully** – Whether eating, walking, or working, do it with full attention

Engaging in daily activities mindfully means being fully present and intentional in whatever you're doing, whether it's eating, walking, working, or even washing dishes. Here are some simple ways to incorporate mindfulness into your everyday routine:

1. Start Your Day with Intention

- Before getting out of bed, take a few deep breaths.

- Set a positive intention for the day.

2. Mindful Eating

Eat slowly, savoring each bite.Pay attention to the flavors, textures, and smells of your food. Eat food like a water and Drink water like a food. Avoid distractions like TV or scrolling on your phone. Now a days Children wont bite the food without cellphone in their hand . Parents are encouraging this and ts very bad situation .

3. Be Present in Conversations

Listen attentively without thinking about what you'll say next Make eye contact and show genuine interest.

4. Single-Tasking Over Multitasking

Focus on one task at a time instead of juggling multiple things.Give your full attention to what you're doing.

5. Practice Gratitude Throughout the Day

Take moments to appreciate small things—a smile, a breeze, a kind word. Keep a gratitude journal if possible.

6. Move with Awareness

Whether you're walking, stretching, or exercising, notice how your body feels.Take deep breaths and focus on your movements.

7. Mindful Breathing Breaks

Take short pauses throughout the day to breathe deeply and reset. Try the 4-7-8 breathing technique (inhale for 4 seconds, hold for 7, exhale for 8).

8. End Your Day with Reflection

Before bed, reflect on what went well during the day .Release any stress or tension with a few deep breaths.

By practicing mindfulness in your daily activities, you'll experience less stress, greater focus, and a deeper appreciation for life's simple moments.

3. **Limit Distractions** – Reduce multitasking and digital noise to stay more present.

Limiting distractions, especially digital noise and multitasking, is crucial for improving focus and productivity. Here are some strategies to help:

1. Control Digital Distractions

- **Turn Off Notifications** – Silence non-essential notifications on your phone and computer.

- **Use Focus Modes** – Features like "Do Not Disturb" on devices can block interruptions.

- **Limit Social Media** – Use website blockers or apps like Freedom or Cold Turkey.

- **Declutter Your Digital Space** – Organize files and emails to reduce visual noise.

2. Reduce Multitasking

- **Prioritize Tasks** – Focus on one task at a time using techniques like the Pomodoro Technique.

- **Batch Similar Tasks** – Group tasks like emails and calls into specific time blocks.

- **Use a Task Manager** – Apps like To do list or Notion help track progress.

3. Create a Focus-Friendly Environment

•   **Designate a Work Zone** – Keep your workspace clean and distraction-free.

•   **Use Noise-Canceling Headphones** – Play white noise or instrumental music to stay focused.

•   **Set Clear Boundaries** – Let others know your focus time to minimize interruptions.

Would you like specific recommendations for a work or home setting?

4.   **Observe Your Thoughts & Emotions** – Acknowledge thoughts and feelings without getting attached to them.

Observing your thoughts and emotions is a powerful practice that can lead to greater self-awareness, emotional intelligence, and inner peace. Here are some key aspects of this practice:

1. Awareness Without Judgment

•   Notice your thoughts and emotions as they arise, without labeling them as "good" or "bad."

•   Treat them as passing events in your mind rather than absolute truths.

2. Mindfulness and Presence

•   Stay present in the moment instead of getting lost in past regrets or future worries.

- Practices like meditation, deep breathing, or journaling can help cultivate this awareness.

3. Understanding Patterns

- Observe recurring thought patterns or emotional triggers.

- Recognizing these patterns can help you respond more consciously rather than react impulsively.

4. Detachment from Thoughts

- You are not your thoughts; they are just mental events that come and go.

- Instead of identifying with every thought, see them as clouds passing in the sky.

5. Responding vs. Reacting

- By observing your emotions, you create space between stimulus and response.

- This helps in making thoughtful decisions rather than reacting based on impulse.

6. Self-Compassion

- Accept your thoughts and emotions without criticism.

- Being kind to yourself allows for growth and healing.

5. **Cultivate Gratitude** – Appreciate the present moment and what you have.

Cultivating gratitude can transform your mindset, boost happiness, and improve overall well-being. Here are some ways to practice gratitude daily:

1. Keep a Gratitude Journal

- Write down three things you're grateful for each day.

- Be specific (e.g., "I'm grateful for the warm cup of coffee I had this morning" instead of just "I'm grateful for coffee").

I found something interesting when I read the book of Five Champion Questions By Ron Kurtus . These are the five Questions that you can practice in your daily Journal and you can create your daily code of conduct.

The real challenge is that with so much to do , it is easy to allow life to act on you and watch the days quickly slip into weeks , then into momths and finally into years

In my own life I have created what I call my daily code of conduct

What I am thankful for today

What did I learn today

What I did a good job today

Who was I valuable to today

How did I care of myself today

1.   Express Gratitude to Others

One of the incident I can relate to this, when I visited my ElderSons house and I spend couple of days with them . While I was returning back home   My daughter in Law packed me the tiffin for my onward Railway journey.

I reached the station and boarded the train and it was time for open the tiffin box , when I opened there was a small note mentioning –"Thank you so much for your visit and you made us feel so happy and see you again ". I was really overhelmed by this act of expressing gratitude ,

- Say "thank you" often.

- Write a heartfelt note or send a messages to someone you appreciate. Make a practice to keep Gratitude Journal

Here's a simple and heartfelt gratitude message:

"I just want to take a moment to sincerely thank you. Your kindness, support, and generosity truly mean the world to me. I deeply appreciate all that you do, and I'm grateful to have you in my life. Thank you from the bottom of my heart!"

Benefits of Gratitude Journaling

Gratitude journaling is the practice of regularly writing down things you're grateful for. It can have a powerful impact on your mental, emotional, and even physical well-being. Here are some key benefits:

Improves Mental Well-being

Writing about things you appreciate can reduce stress, anxiety, and depression. It shifts your focus from negative thoughts to positive ones.

Example:
"Today, I am grateful for the beautiful sunset I saw on my evening walk. It made me feel calm and peaceful."

Enhances Positivity and Happiness

By focusing on gratitude, you train your mind to recognize the good in your life, leading to an overall happier mindset.

Example:

"I am thankful for my supportive family and the laughter we shared over dinner today."

Strengthens Relationships

Expressing gratitude towards others fosters deeper connections and appreciation in relationships.

Example:

"I appreciate my friend for checking in on me when I was feeling low today. It made me feel loved."

Boosts Self-Esteem

Acknowledging your achievements and good moments helps you feel more confident and fulfilled.

Example:

"I am grateful for my dedication to my work today. I completed a difficult task, and it felt rewarding."

Improves Sleep Quality

Writing about positive experiences before bed can lead to better sleep and a more restful mind.

Example:

"I'm thankful for the cozy blanket and a good book that helped me unwind tonight."

Encourages Mindfulness

Gratitude journaling keeps you present and mindful, reducing overthinking and worry.

Example:

"I truly enjoyed my cup of coffee this morning, savoring every sip and feeling grateful   for the quiet moment."

Increases Resilience

Gratitude helps you focus on the positives even in tough times, making you more resilient.

Example:

"Despite a challenging day at work, I am grateful for the lesson I learned and the strength I gained from it."

Living In Gratitude is a way to be a peace- Dada J.P Wasawani

Wife and mother of Four Children sighed as she faced the Kitchen sink after the dinner It was overflowing with dirty dishes which she had to wash, dry and put away. Suddenly, she remembered the lines she had heard as a child, "Thank god for dirty dishes, they have a tale to tell : While other folks go hungry , we are eating pretty well. With home and health and happiness, we shouldn't want to fuss; for by this stack of evidence

God is very good to us.

Count your blessing and thank god for every living moment, for God's generosity to you is infinite.

Why should i be grateful? most of us would agree that complaining and criticising can make life better and sour , while being grateful makes us positive, happy and optimistic; it help us to see the bright side of life. It teaches us the art of appreciation. Some experts believe that we lack the spirit of gratitude because we take things for granted. The street Urchin into whose hands you drop a packet of biscuit look up at you with a smile.

He has known what is to be hungry. He knows the value of those biscuits . What do we do when someone takes the trouble to shop and plan and cook and clean , so that a place of hot food is put before us at regular intervals ?, we make faces and complain that the dish is either too spicy or not spicy enough . that is boring; it is not our favourite recipe that has been served; and that the vegetables on the plate are the not the ones we like.

May be we need to go without things we take for granted,to be able to appreciate what we have . Now give me one good reason why we should allow ourselves to go through a loss just to realise the value of what we already have ?

When you become aware of all that you have to be grateful for . when actually begin to count your blessings. You will be overwhelmed with gratitude for all that God has bestowed on you so unstintingly. your peaceful sleep, your loved once whose dearest wish in just to see you happy , your friends who add value to your life , your good health which you utterly fail to appreciate untill you fail ill, the fresh air and sunlight around you , the marvels of technology which have made our life so easy, society and community which let you live in peace and order- where you would be without them all .

Let us thank God for sorrow – It teaches us pity and compassion. Let us thank god for pain and illness – we learn forbearance and patience. Let us thank God for friends who let us down and hurt us – for we learn the Devine quality of forgiveness there from.Let us thank god for suffering – It teaches us courage . Let us thank god for disappointments – for they teach us to be ready his appointment.

When we thank Lord all the time . we build ourselves a ladder of consciousness on which we can climb and touch the very pinnacle of peace.

3. Practice Mindfulness

•   Take a moment to appreciate the present moment. I remember one of the mindfull meditation class which I attended and our Teacher made us to sit with closed eyes putting one hand on your chest and one hand on our Lap . just told us to remember the days of Happiest moments you witnessed from our child hood to this period of time . remember one by one, For example May be the best gift you received from your parents , May be the Very good marks you received in your adamic ., May be you have first met your soulmate , May be first salary you earned from your job and given to your parents , May be your memories of outing with your friends   Whatever the happiest moment you ever come across just think and visualise . After this session we were so happy and blissful and I felt my mind was so calm . We always think what was the worst things happened to us in our life instead of remembering the best moments

•   Notice the beauty in small things—sunlight, a smile, nature.

4. Reframe Challenges as Lessons

•   Instead of dwelling on difficulties, ask yourself, "What can I learn from this?"

•   Find the silver lining in tough situations.

5. Start and End Your Day with Gratitude

•   When you wake up, think of one thing you're looking forward to.

- Before bed, reflect on the best part of your day.

6. **Connect with Nature** – Spend time outdoors to ground yourself in the present.

Connecting with nature is one of the best ways to refresh your mind, body, and soul. Whether you prefer an adventurous hike, a peaceful walk in the park, or simply listening to the rain from your window, there are countless ways to immerse yourself in the natural world.

The Sage and the Golden Bow IIn the ancient city of Varanasi, nestled on the banks of the sacred Ganges, lived a wise sage named Rishi Devadatta. People traveled from far and wide to seek his guidance, for his wisdom was renowned across the land. Despite being revered, he led a simple life, living in a modest hut and meditating under an old banyan tree.

One day, a wealthy merchant named Dhanananda came to visit the sage. He carried with him a gleaming golden bowl encrusted with precious gems. Bowing before the sage, he said, "O Wise One, I have everything a man could desire—wealth, power, and luxury—yet my mind is restless. I am constantly worried about my possessions, my reputation, and the future. Please guide me toward peace."

The sage smiled and asked the merchant to stay with him for a few days. Dhanananda, though hesitant at first, agreed. Over the next few days, he observed the sage's way of living— eating simple food, sleeping under the stars, and remaining content with whatever he had. Yet, the sage's face glowed with peace and joy.

One evening, the sage handed the golden bowl back to the merchant and said, "Take this back with you."

Dhanananda was puzzled. "But you didn't even use it, O Sage."

The sage chuckled. "Tell me, Dhanananda, how did you feel these past few days without your luxurious belongings?"

The merchant pondered and replied, "At first, I was uneasy, but soon, I felt light and free. I had no worries about guarding my wealth, no fear of losing anything. I felt at peace."

The sage nodded. "You see, true peace is not in what you possess, but in how free you are from attachments. Your mind clings to wealth, and that attachment creates anxiety. A golden bowl, no matter how valuable, is still just a bowl. It does not make your food taste better or nourish your soul. Mindful living is about cherishing the present, being aware of your thoughts, and freeing yourself from unnecessary burdens."

Dhanananda bowed deeply before the sage. He finally understood that wealth was not the cause of his unrest, but his attachment to it. From that day onward, he lived with awareness, enjoying his riches without letting them control his peace.

The lesson of the sage spread far and wide, reminding people that true mindfulness is about detachment, awareness, and living fully in the present.

This story is inspired by teachings from the Bhagavad Gita and Buddhist philosophy, emphasizing detachment, inner peace, and mindful living.

Chapter 5: Overcoming Self Judgement and Comparison

"You wouldn't worry so much about what others think of you if you realized how seldom they do."

— Eleanor Roosevelt

In a world where we are constantly bombarded with images of success, beauty, and perfection, it is easy to fall into the trap of self-judgment and comparison. The mind becomes a battlefield, questioning our worth, abilities, and progress. We measure ourselves against curated highlight reels, forgetting that behind every perfect picture and every success story lies a journey of struggle, failure, and resilience.

Self-judgment is a silent thief, robbing us of our confidence, joy, and inner peace. It whispers words of doubt, convincing us that we are not enough. It magnifies our flaws while diminishing our strengths. But what if we choose to silence that voice? What if we decide to embrace ourselves as we are, understanding that growth is a process and that perfection is an illusion?

Comparison, too, is a dangerous game. When we compare our journey to that of others, we discount our uniqueness. We were not created to walk the same path as anyone else. Our struggles, our triumphs, our pace—all are uniquely ours. The moment we stop looking outward for validation and turn inward for self-acceptance, we reclaim our power.

Overcoming self-judgment and comparison begins with self-awareness. We must catch ourselves in the act of negative self-talk and reframe our thoughts with kindness. We must celebrate our progress, no matter how small, and appreciate the person we are becoming. Gratitude shifts our perspective, allowing us to see our own blessings rather than longing for someone else's.

One of the greatest acts of self-liberation is to realize that we are enough as we are. We do not need external validation to define our worth. We do not need to outshine others to be worthy of success. Our value is inherent. When we embrace this truth, we step into a life of confidence, authenticity, and true fulfillment.

It is time to free ourselves from the chains of self-judgment and comparison. It is time to walk boldly in our journey, knowing that our path is uniquely designed for us. The moment we release unrealistic expectations and self-criticism, we unlock the door to inner peace, happiness, and limitless possibilities.

DREAMING , Sleeping, walking and Beyond

The word as Adi Shankaracharya said is a Myth that keeps on changing A lady came to Ramana Maharshi and said that she perceives the world very clearly. The relations i maintain with the family, the society and the world appears very real and how can i call them a myth ? Ramana Maharshi replied was the world there when you are asleep? Did the mind or body , by which you perceived the world, exist when you were sleeping?

What appears and disappears is not real . You who exist in all states are real . You who are conscious enough while awake and remotely conscious even during deep sleep and dreaming are real .

Mind and body are the elements that distance the individual from real nature .Mind is the source of all diverse thoughts. It creats the false notion of " I' or Ego. It turns ones attention towards the illusory world outside and creates desire. When the desires are not fulfilled the mind becomes tense. In short it is during the waking state when the mind is active, the happiness gets lost and it is during the deep sleep state when the mind or world are absent, the real happiness is gained.

When one goes to sleep, gradually the body awreness goes. Sushipti, deep sleep, the state in which there is no mind, body or the world, is one's natuaral state, the state of true happiness. But deep sleep is interrupted by waking state and one comes under the domain of his mind, body and the world and losses the happiness in the process.

King Janaka was fast asleep on his royal bed. Suddenly the neighbouring country invaded his kingdom and took him as prisoner. Having been let off, he found himself in the street, begging for food. When he got up , he realised that it was all a dream.

The dream experiences disturbed him and pondered over the question of what is real .He then went to sage Ashtavakra and said , My Dream experience appeared real and my waking experience too appeared real . Advise me what my real Nature is? The sage repplied " Niether the state of begger on the street nor the state of King is Real . You are the Real , You who are consciuos in all the states of waking , dream and deep sleep state are real , realise your True self .

Normally, the individual think that on waking up from dream , he is back to reality but according to Ramans Maharshi , he has only come from one unreal world to another unreal world. There is no difference between the images that one seas in dreams and images of the world that he sees during the waking state.

During the waking state it is day dream and during the dream state it is night dream . The only difference is the dream last for a short while the waking last for longer. Both are unreal and both are creation of the mind.

Arise , Awake ", says Katha upanishad. The real awakening is sleeping in relation with the world and waking is reaction to the self. It means transcending oneself from all the three states and realising the self in the fourth state of Turiya.

The power of Mindset and Personal Growth

The Power of Mindset

Your mindset is the foundation of everything you do. It shapes your perception of the world, influences your decisions, and determines your success or failure. A growth mindset, as opposed to a fixed mindset, allows you to embrace challenges, persist through obstacles, and continuously improve.

The Difference Between Fixed and Growth Mindsets

- **Fixed Mindset**: People with a fixed mindset believe their abilities, intelligence, and talents are static. They avoid challenges, fear failure, and view effort as fruitless.

- **Growth Mindset**: Those with a growth mindset believe abilities can be developed through dedication and hard work. They embrace challenges, learn from criticism, and persist despite setbacks.

Steps to Cultivate a Growth Mindset

Embrace Challenges – See difficulties as opportunities to grow rather than obstacles.

Learn from Criticism – Use feedback to improve rather than take it personally.

Develop Resilience – Understand that failure is a stepping stone to success.

Commit to Lifelong Learning – Continuously seek knowledge and self-improvement.

1. **Surround Yourself with Growth-Oriented People** – Be in an environment that encourages learning and progress.

Personal Growth: The Journey to Becoming Your Best Self

"A man without a smiling face must not open a shop " - Chinese Proverb

Personal growth is a lifelong journey. It involves self-reflection, setting meaningful goals, and taking consistent action toward self-improvement. It requires developing mental strength, emotional intelligence, and a strong sense of purpose. Live life like there is no tomorrow and achieve the best within you , love the people around in your life . Live a high volume life , take risk , reach high , be authentic and great. Do your job with passision and braver and with sparkle in your eye. Do it all with the intensity .

Strategies for Personal Growth

- **Set Clear Goals**: Define what success looks like for you.

- **Adopt a Positive Mindset**: Focus on possibilities rather than limitations.

- **Take Responsibility**: Own your actions and decisions.

- **Step Out of Your Comfort Zone**: Growth happens when you challenge yourself.

- **Practice Self-Discipline**: Stay committed to your goals and resist distractions.

- **Seek Mentorship and Guidance**: Learn from those who have walked the path before you.

Conclusion

Mindset and personal growth go hand in hand. By shifting to a growth-oriented mindset and actively pursuing personal development, you unlock your true potential and create a fulfilling and successful life. The journey may not always be easy, but the rewards of self-improvement are limitless.

Start today—one small step at a time.

Overcoming Negative Patterns

Overcoming negative patterns takes awareness, effort, and persistence. Whether it's negative thinking, self-sabotage, unhealthy habits, or toxic relationships, here are some steps to break free:

1. Identify the Pattern

- What keeps happening in your life that you want to change?

- Is there a common trigger or emotional state that leads to it?

- Are there any limiting beliefs fueling this pattern?

2. Understand the Root Cause

- When did this pattern start?

- Is it linked to past experiences, fears, or insecurities?

- Does it serve a hidden purpose (comfort, avoidance, etc.)?

3. Challenge Negative Thoughts

- Notice self-defeating thoughts and replace them with positive, realistic ones.

- Use affirmations or cognitive reframing to shift your mindset.

4. Change Your Response

- If you normally react with avoidance, try facing the issue.

- If you engage in negative self-talk, practice self-compassion.

- If you repeat toxic relationship patterns, set boundaries.

. Replace with Positive Habits

- Swap unhealthy coping mechanisms for healthier alternatives.

- Develop routines that support your goals.

- Surround yourself with people who uplift you.

Practice Mindfulness & Self-Awareness

- Journaling, meditation, or therapy can help track your progress.

- Observe your thoughts without judgment and stay present.

Seek Support

- Talk to a friend, mentor, or therapist for guidance.

- Join a group or community that encourages personal growth.

Stay Persistent & Patient

- Breaking patterns takes time—don't be too hard on yourself.

- Celebrate small wins and learn from setbacks.

Confidence and self-love are deeply connected. When you truly appreciate yourself, your confidence naturally grows. Here are some key insights and practices to build both:

3. Understanding Confidence & Self-Love

- Confidence is believing in your abilities and worth. It comes from experience, self-trust, and positive reinforcement.

- Self-love is accepting yourself as you are, flaws and all. It means treating yourself with kindness and respect.

Ways to Build Confidence

- Step Outside Your Comfort Zone – Growth happens when you challenge yourself.

- Practice Self-Compassion – Talk to yourself like you would to a friend.

- Celebrate Small Wins – Every achievement counts, no matter how small.

- Develop a Growth Mindset – See failures as lessons, not as proof you're not good enough.

- Improve Your Posture & Body Language – Stand tall, make eye contact, and carry yourself with assurance.

3. Ways to Cultivate Self-Love

Stop Comparing Yourself to Others – Your journey is unique.

- Set Boundaries – Protect your time, energy, and emotions.

- Practice Gratitude – Appreciate what you have and who you are.

- Surround Yourself with Positivity – Choose relationships that uplift and support you.

- Do Things That Bring You Joy – Prioritize your happiness and well-being.

Here are some affirmations for self-love:

I am enough, just as I am.

I deserve love, kindness, and respect—especially from myself.

I embrace my flaws and imperfections; they make me unique and beautiful.

I choose to treat myself with the same compassion I give to others.

Perspective Shift

A perspective shift refers to a change in the way a person views a situation, belief, or concept. It can be intentional or unintentional and often leads to new insights, growth, or problem-solving.

Here are some key points and notes on Perspective Shift

Key Aspects of Perspective Shift

Cognitive Flexibility – The ability to see things from multiple viewpoints.

Emotional Intelligence – Recognizing and managing emotions to understand others' perspectives.

Empathy – Putting oneself in another's shoes to gain insight into their experiences.

Open-Mindedness – Being willing to challenge existing beliefs and consider alternative viewpoints.

Awareness & Reflection – Observing thoughts, behaviors, and biases to identify areas for growth.

Causes of Perspective Shift

•	New Experiences (travel, meeting new people, learning new skills)

•	Education & Knowledge (reading, studying, exposure to new ideas)

•	Difficult Situations (failure, adversity, loss, or major life changes)

•	Personal Growth & Mindfulness (meditation, therapy, journaling)

•	Conversations & Debates (engaging in discussions that challenge beliefs)

Benefits of a Perspective Shift

•	Improves Decision-Making – Seeing multiple sides of a problem helps in better solutions.

•	Enhances Relationships – Understanding different viewpoints fosters empathy and connection.

•	Reduces Stress & Conflict – A broader perspective can reduce rigid thinking and ease tensions.

•	Boosts Creativity – Looking at things differently leads to innovative ideas.

•	Encourages Growth & Adaptability – Makes a person more resilient and open to **change.**

How to Cultivate a Perspective Shift

Practice Active Listening – Focus on truly understanding before responding.

Ask Thought-Provoking Questions – Challenge your assumptions and beliefs.

Expose Yourself to Diversity – Read, travel, and interact with people from different backgrounds.

Reflect & Journal – Write down thoughts and analyze patterns in thinking.

Engage in Role Reversal – Imagine yourself in another person's position.

Seek Feedback – Ask others how they view situations differently.

Embrace Change – Accept uncertainty and be willing to adjust your mindset.

The Mirror's Truth

Mira had always been her worst critic. Every morning, she stood in front of the mirror, adjusting her hair, frowning at imaginary flaws, and sighing at the reflection that never seemed "good enough."

One day, her grandmother handed her an old, dusty mirror. "This," she said, "is not just any mirror. It shows you not how you look, but how you see yourself."

Curious, Mira peered into the glass. To her surprise, she saw a version of herself—tired, doubtful, weighed down by the expectations she had set.

She gasped. "This can't be real!"

Her grandmother smiled. "What you see is shaped by what you believe about yourself. If you always tell yourself you're not enough, that's all you'll ever see."

Determined, Mira decided to change the way she spoke to herself. She replaced self-criticism with kindness. Instead of saying, "I wish I looked different," she said, "I am unique in my own way." Instead of thinking, "I'm not good enough," she reminded herself, "I am capable and strong."

Weeks passed, and each time she looked into the mirror, the reflection grew brighter. Her posture straightened, her eyes sparkled, and her smile came effortlessly. The mirror had not changed—she had.

One day, she no longer needed the special mirror to see her worth. She realized that confidence and self-love had been inside her all along.

And from that day forward, she carried her real mirror—the one in her heart—with pride.

Moral: The way you see yourself shapes your reality. Speak kindly to yourself, believe in your worth, and watch how your reflection changes.

Chapter 6: How Digital Age Controls You

"In an age of infinite information, wisdom is knowing what to ignore."

– James Clear

The digital age has given us incredible access to information, entertainment, and communication, but it also comes with hidden mechanisms that subtly shape our thoughts, behaviors, and decisions. Here's how the digital world controls your mind:

1. Social Media Manipulation

• Platforms like Facebook, Instagram, and TikTok use algorithms to show content that keeps you engaged, often prioritizing emotional or controversial posts.

• Dopamine hits from likes, shares, and comments create addictive feedback loops.

• Echo chambers reinforce existing beliefs, making it harder to see other perspectives.

2. Personalized Content & AI Algorithms

• AI-driven recommendations (YouTube, Netflix, etc.) create filter bubbles, showing only content that aligns with your interests, limiting diverse viewpoints.

- The more time you spend online, the better algorithms understand your preferences, keeping you hooked.

3. News & Information Manipulation

- Clickbait headlines and sensational news shape opinions before facts are verified.

- Fake news and deepfakes spread rapidly, making it hard to distinguish truth from fiction.

- Biased search engine results influence what information you see first.

4. Surveillance & Data Tracking

- Your online behavior is constantly tracked, creating psychological profiles used for targeted advertising and political influence.

- Companies use dark patterns (e.g., infinite scrolling, autoplay) to keep you engaged longer than intended.

5. Addiction & Mental Health Impact

- Smartphone addiction disrupts focus, productivity, and sleep.

- Comparison culture on social media fuels anxiety, depression, and low self-esteem.

- Fear of missing out (FOMO) keeps users compulsively checking their devices.

6. AI-Generated Content & Deepfakes

- AI-generated news, videos, and voice clones can manipulate reality.

- People are more susceptible to misinformation as AI-generated content becomes more convincing.

How to Regain Control

- Limit screen time: Use digital wellness tools to reduce social media and smartphone usage.

- Be mindful of algorithms: Recognize when you're being influenced and seek alternative sources.

- Diversify content consumption: Follow a range of sources for balanced perspectives.

- Protect your data: Use privacy settings, ad blockers, and VPNs to limit tracking.

- Practice digital detox: Take regular breaks from digital devices to regain focus and mental clarity.

The digital age is powerful, but awareness is key. Once you understand how it influences your mind, you can take steps to reclaim control

Some important tips to the younger generation

Be the Master, Not the Puppet

- Use technology as a tool, not a trap. Don't let screens dictate how you feel or what you do.

- Remember, you *control* your devices—they don't control you.

Limit Screen Time

- Set daily limits on social media, gaming, and videos.

- Take breaks—at least 10-15 minutes every hour—to rest your eyes and mind.

Think Before You Click

- Not everything online is true. Always question what you see.

- Be mindful of what you share—once it's online, it's hard to take back.

Protect Your Privacy

- Never share personal information with strangers online.

- Be cautious about clicking on suspicious links or accepting friend requests from people you don't know.

Prioritize Real-Life Connections

- Spend time with family and friends without screens.

- Play outside, read books, and enjoy hobbies that don't involve technology.

Recognize the Signs of Digital Addiction

•   If you feel anxious, sad, or restless without your phone, take a step back.

•   If scrolling replaces sleep, homework, or family time, it's time to unplug.

Learn Digital Balance

•   Technology is amazing, but balance is key.

•   Use it to create, learn, and grow—not just to consume endlessly.

The digital world is powerful, but real life is even more beautiful. Enjoy both—wisely! 😊

The Puppeteer's Strings – How the digital age is rewiring your brain based on one article

Ethan groggily reached for his phone the moment his eyes fluttered open. The blue glow of the screen bathed his face as he scrolled through notifications—news alerts, emails, messages.

His heart rate spiked when he saw a breaking headline: *"New Cybersecurity Breach Exposes Millions."* A shiver ran down his spine, but his thumb continued its unconscious dance across the screen.

His morning routine had become a ritual dictated by the digital world. A playlist auto-selected his mood for the day, an app calculated his ideal breakfast, and his smartwatch reminded him to stretch. At work, algorithms curated his tasks, suggested responses to emails, and even predicted when he needed a break—though he rarely took one.

One evening, while out with friends, Ethan noticed something odd. The conversation had lulled, and everyone's eyes were glued to their devices. Even laughter felt artificial, as if dictated by viral trends rather than genuine joy.

He glanced down at his own phone—an alert from his newsfeed: *"How the Digital Age is Rewiring Your Brain."* He scoffed but clicked on it anyway.

The article spoke of a silent puppeteer—an invisible force shaping thoughts, habits, and choices through data-driven manipulation.

It described how social media kept people addicted, how notifications controlled emotions, and how even personal beliefs could be influenced by the content fed to them.

Ethan set his phone down, suddenly uneasy. He thought back to a time before everything was dictated by algorithms. A time when decisions felt *his*. Was he living, or merely existing in a script written by unseen hands?

Determined, he silenced his phone for the first time in years and stepped outside.

The city was alive, yet eerily quiet without the digital noise. He took a deep breath, letting reality—true reality—wash over him. The question lingered: *Was he free, or had he only just realized the cage?*

And somewhere, in a data center miles away, an algorithm recalibrated, searching for a new way to pull him back in.

CHAPTER 7: THE POWER OF INTUITION AND GUT FEELING

"Intuition is the whisper of the soul, guiding us where logic cannot."

The power of intuition and gut feeling is often underestimated, but it plays a significant role in decision-making, problem-solving, and even creativity. Intuition is that deep, instinctive knowing that arises without conscious reasoning. It's like a subconscious superpower that helps you make quick, effective decisions, often based on past experiences and pattern recognition.

Let Me narrate a True Story , rather than a metaphor , too debunk the Myth of man being intrinsically violent.

An Old Buddha Statue was moved from its old site to its present location in the Wat TriMet temple in Bangkok in 1957. The big Statue fell of the crane and sustained a crack < Further work was suspended untill the following day.

An anxious monk , who came in the night to check the damage, shone a torch on the crack and found to his surprise that light reflected from the cracked area. A little chipping of the mud revealed that the Budha was made of pure gold but covered in hard clay

It wieghed over 5 tones , The 700 year old Budha had covered in mud to hide from the marauding Burmese army a few century ago and nobody seemed to remember that the strong clay was only an exterior and it concealed something precious.

This is the universal truth about . Within the clay exterior is golden Buddha. That is who we are The Golden Buddha is a metaphor for the inherent goodness we are imbued with . Man is basically good, but crcumstances do not always allow him to retain his intrinsic goodness.

Studying Criminology Political scientist James Wilson and Psychologist Richard Herrnstein too averred that human are not criminals by birth but are slaves to circumstances. As Urdu Poet Irfaan Peshawari put it Like this .

No one is evil by birth / Nor is everyone equally so good / circustances change humans/ none is greater than the fate .

We have the Immense possibilities and potential to become good because goodness is a basic human trait . Rabindranath Tagore Wrote in Gitanjali — Every infant come with adevine message that God is not yet discouraged of Man . Yes God is not yet despondent of man because He knows that sooner or Later , man will realise and discover sooner or later discover the goodness he is born with .

We all have noble qualities , but we are not often alive to them . Lets zeroin on those postive attributes and make the world a far metter and desirable to live in . Because what you give energy to , is what gets enhanced .

Why Intuition Matters

1. **Faster Decision-Making** – Intuition allows you to make split-second choices without overanalyzing.

2. **Emotional Intelligence** – It helps in reading people and situations, which is crucial in relationships and business.Emotional Intelligence (EI) refers to the ability to recognize, understand, manage, and influence emotions in oneself and others. Coined by psychologists Peter Salovey and John Mayer and popularized by Daniel Goleman, EI has become a crucial factor in personal development, leadership, and workplace effectiveness.

Feed the right Emotion -In life , both faith and fear will arise within you and you choose which one will prevail . The thing is both of these emotions will always be present within you The emotions you continually feed is that will dominate your life . You cant expect your fear simply to disappear If you continuously focus on your fear , entertain them , they will increase . Don't feed them with gossip or negative news shows of frieghtening movies . Focus on your faith and feed it .

Components of Emotional Intelligence

According to Goleman, EI consists of five key components:

1. **Self-Awareness** – The ability to recognize and understand one's emotions and their impact on thoughts and behavior.

2. **Self-Regulation** – The capacity to control emotional reactions, adapt to change, and manage impulses effectively.

3.   **Motivation** – The drive to achieve goals with passion, resilience, and a positive mindset.

4.   **Empathy** – The ability to understand and share the feelings of others, fostering strong interpersonal relationships.

5. **Social Skills** – The proficiency in managing relationships, communicating effectively, and resolving conflicts.

Importance of Emotional Intelligence

EI plays a vital role in various aspects of life, including:

- **Personal Growth** – Enhances self-awareness, self-control, and emotional well-being.

- **Professional Success** – Helps in leadership, teamwork, and decision-making.

- **Relationships** – Strengthens communication, trust, and understanding in personal and professional settings.

- **Conflict Resolution** – Aids in managing disagreements and finding constructive solutions.

Developing Emotional Intelligence

Enhancing EI requires conscious effort and practice. Strategies include:

- **Mindfulness and Reflection** – Regular self-assessment and mindfulness exercises improve self-awareness.

- **Active Listening** – Paying close attention to others' emotions and perspectives fosters empathy.

- **Effective Communication** – Expressing emotions constructively enhances interpersonal skills.

- **Stress Management** – Learning to handle pressure and emotions positively promotes self-regulation.

- **Continuous Learning** – Seeking feedback and engaging in personal development activities strengthens EI.

Conclusion

Emotional Intelligence is a powerful skill that influences personal happiness and professional success. By developing self-awareness, empathy, and effective communication, individuals can build stronger relationships, enhance leadership abilities, and navigate life's challenges more effectively. Cultivating EI is a lifelong process that fosters resilience, adaptability, and overall well-being.

Creativity & Innovation – Many great ideas and breakthroughs come from a "gut feeling" rather than logic alone.

Survival Instinct – Historically, intuition has been vital for human survival, warning of danger before logic can process it.

Alignment with Purpose – Often, intuition nudges you toward things that align with your true self, helping you stay on the right path.

How to Strengthen Your Intuition

- **Listen to Your Gut** – Pay attention to physical sensations and subtle feelings.

- **Meditation & Mindfulness** – A quiet mind hears intuition more clearly.

- **Journaling** – Write about your feelings and choices; patterns will emerge.

- **Trust It & Test It** – Follow your instincts on small things and see how often you're right.

- **Reduce Overthinking** – Logic is important, but sometimes, too much analysis blocks intuition.

Intuition isn't magical—it's your subconscious mind processing information faster than your conscious mind can. The key is learning to trust and refine it. Have you had moments where intuition led you to the right decision?

The Story of King Janaka and Ashtavakra

King Janaka, the ruler of Mithila, was not only a mighty king but also a great seeker of wisdom. He often held philosophical discussions with learned sages. However, despite all his knowledge, he felt something was missing—an inner knowing, a deep intuition that would guide him beyond logic.

One day, he announced in his court, **"Whoever can truly enlighten me on the nature of reality and intuition shall be rewarded."** Many scholars and sages came forward, debating and presenting their arguments, but none satisfied the king.

Hearing about this, a young boy named **Ashtavakra**, who was deformed with eight bends in his body, arrived at the court. Seeing his appearance, the courtiers laughed. But Ashtavakra remained calm and smiled.

He said, **"O King, why do you seek wisdom from those who cannot even see beyond appearances? True knowledge and intuition come from within, not from external debates."**

Intrigued, King Janaka invited him for a discourse.

Ashtavakra then asked, **"If right now, a fire were to break out in this palace, what would you do?"**

The king replied, **"I would immediately escape to save my life."**

Ashtavakra smiled, **"You did not stop to think or analyze. Your gut feeling told you to escape. That is intuition! It is immediate, beyond logic. The same way, deep wisdom does not come from endless debates but from an inner realization."**

Realizing the truth in his words, King Janaka asked, **"How can I develop this deep intuition?"**

Ashtavakra replied, **"By silencing the noise of the mind and trusting the wisdom within. When you stop**

seeking externally, the answers will emerge from within you."

From that day onward, King Janaka practiced deep meditation and mindfulness, ultimately becoming an enlightened ruler, guided by his powerful intuition.

Moral of the Story:

• Intuition is a deep inner knowing beyond logic and reasoning.

• True wisdom does not come from external sources but from within.

• Silence and self-awareness help in strengthening gut feelings and intuitive power.

This story from the **Ashtavakra Gita** beautifully illustrates how intuition, when nurtured, can be a guiding force in life.

Chapter 8: The Path of Personal Mastery

"We are what we repeatedly do. Excellence, then, is not an act, but a habit."

- Aristotle

The **Path of Personal Mastery** is a lifelong journey of self-discovery, growth, and self-improvement. It involves cultivating self-awareness, developing skills, and striving for excellence in all areas of life. It's not about perfection but about continuous learning, discipline, and intentionality.

Two beautiful words Personal Mastery. They have an inspirational vibe to them. They offer hope, challenge. provoke, the vision, they affirm – and remind of our highest possibilities. Each of us go into the world and live our best life as much as possible. Sometimes doesn't seem always fair

To be given the gift of life is to be given an awesome responsibility. We will encounter all type of difficulties , we will face hard and confusing time as well . that is how the life happens. But , At the same time life offers you daily opportunity to shine . To polish your gifts , to release your chains , to achieve your personal mastery.

Make a firm commitment today that will alter the course of your life . Forever dedicate yourself to personal mastery . Think about your own thinking , detect your authentic values and what you ain to stand for. How can you be who you are if you do not know your real values . Focus on your personal gain human potential . Learn to let go the emotional baggage which you are carrying for the long. Refuse to tolerate the negetivity in life

Key Elements of Personal Mastery

1.   **Self-Awareness** – Understanding your strengths, weaknesses, emotions, values, and purpose. Practicing mindfulness, journaling, seeking feedback, and self-reflection are some ways to improve self-awareness. The more you know yourself, the better you can align your actions with your goals and values.

2.   **Vision & Purpose** – Having a clear goal or purpose that aligns with your values and drives your actions.

Vision is the guiding force that shapes our aspirations and long-term goals. It provides clarity, direction, and motivation, acting as a compass in our personal mastery journey. A strong vision allows us to see beyond challenges and remain committed to growth and excellence.

Purpose is the deeper reason behind our efforts—the "why" that fuels our passion and persistence. It gives meaning to our pursuits, aligning our actions with our values and aspirations. When purpose is clear, personal mastery becomes a fulfilling journey rather than just a destination.

By cultivating both vision and purpose, we create a life of continuous improvement, self-awareness, and intentional progress.

Personal mastery is not about perfection but about the commitment to lifelong learning and self-betterment.

Insight on Vision and Purpose

Vision and **purpose** are two fundamental elements that shape our personal and professional lives. While they are interconnected, they serve distinct roles in guiding us toward fulfillment and success.

Vision: The Big Picture

Vision is about seeing the future before it happens. It provides direction, inspiration, and clarity about where we want to go. A strong vision acts as a guiding star, keeping us motivated even in challenging times.

Key aspects of vision:

- Future-oriented: It paints a picture of what you aspire to achieve.

- Inspiring: A compelling vision energizes and motivates.

- Directional: It provides a sense of focus and helps with decision-making.

Example:
A company's vision might be *"To create a world where sustainable energy powers every home."* On a personal level, your vision could be *"To inspire and empower people through education and mentorship."*

Purpose: The Reason Behind the Journey

Purpose is the *why* behind what you do. It gives meaning to your actions and keeps you grounded. Without purpose, even the clearest vision can feel empty or directionless.

Key aspects of purpose:

- Rooted in values: It aligns with your beliefs and passions.

- Meaningful: It makes your work and life fulfilling.

- Action-driven: It fuels your daily efforts.

Example:
A purpose-driven company might say, *"We exist to make clean energy accessible to all."*

On a personal level, your purpose could be *"To help others unlock their potential and achieve their dreams."*

The Connection Between Vision and Purpose

- **Vision** is where you're going.

- **Purpose** is why you're going there.

When your vision and purpose are aligned, you move forward with clarity, resilience, and passion. A strong purpose sustains motivation, and a clear vision keeps you on track.

How to Define Your Vision and Purpose

1. **Reflect on What Matters** – What excites and inspires you? What impact do you want to have?

2. **Identify Your Strengths** – What are you naturally good at? What skills or talents can you use?

3. **Think About the Legacy You Want to Leave** – What do you want to be remembered for?

Alfred Nobel: The Story of His Legacy

Alfred Nobel (1833–1896) was a Swedish chemist, engineer, and inventor best known for inventing dynamite. However, his true legacy lies in the Nobel Prizes, which were established after his death and continue to honor outstanding achievements in science, literature, and peace.

Early Life and Inventions

Nobel was born in Stockholm, Sweden, into a family of inventors. His father, Immanuel Nobel, was an engineer and industrialist who worked with explosives. Alfred showed a natural aptitude for science and engineering, eventually studying chemistry in Paris.

In 1867, he invented dynamite, a more stable and safer alternative to nitroglycerin. This invention revolutionized construction and mining, making Nobel immensely wealthy. He later developed more explosive compounds and held over 350 patents.

A Shocking Wake-Up Call

In 1888, a French newspaper mistakenly published an obituary for Alfred Nobel instead of his deceased brother Ludvig. The obituary was titled **"The Merchant of Death is**

Dead" and condemned Nobel for making his fortune from explosives used in warfare.

This deeply affected Nobel, making him rethink his legacy. Determined to be remembered for something positive, he decided to leave the majority of his fortune to establish the Nobel Prizes.

The Nobel Prize and His Lasting Impact

In his will, Nobel allocated his wealth to fund annual prizes in **Physics, Chemistry, Medicine, Literature, and Peace** (later, the Nobel Memorial Prize in Economic Sciences was added). His goal was to reward those who contributed to the betterment of humanity.

Since 1901, the **Nobel Prizes** have been awarded to individuals and organizations that have made groundbreaking contributions in their respective fields. The **Nobel Peace Prize**, in particular, honors those who promote peace and resolve conflicts worldwide.

Legacy

Despite his association with explosives, Alfred Nobel is now remembered a visionary who transformed his wealth into a force for global good. His story is a powerful example of how one person can redefine their legacy.

Write It Down – Clarify your vision and purpose in simple yet powerful statements.Make journal and write your goal daily and read it once which will embedded in your mind and you will start taking action

Live It Daily – Align your actions, decisions, and goals with your vision and purpose.

When you have a compelling vision and a strong sense of purpose, you wake up each day with intention and drive. These elements shape the way you lead, create, and contribute to the world

3.   **Discipline & Consistency** – Developing daily habits and routines that support your growth.

Discipline and consistency are the foundation of success in any area of life. Discipline helps you stay committed to your goals, even when motivation fades. It requires self-control, determination, and the ability to push through challenges.

Consistency, on the other hand, ensures steady progress. Small, repeated actions over time lead to significant results. It is not about perfection but about showing up every day and making an effort.

Together, discipline and consistency create a powerful formula for personal growth, success, and resilience. Stay focused, take small steps daily, and trust the process!

Emotional Intelligence – Managing emotions, building resilience, and fostering strong relationships. motional intelligence (EI) is the ability to recognize, understand, and manage your own emotions while also being able to perceive and influence the emotions of others. Managing EI effectively involves:

Self-Awareness – Recognize your emotions and their impact on your thoughts and behavior.

Self-Regulation – Control impulsive reactions, stay adaptable, and manage stress effectively.

Motivation – Maintain a positive attitude and stay driven toward goals despite challenges.

Empathy – Understand and consider others' emotions to build strong relationships.

Social Skills – Communicate clearly, manage conflicts wisely, and foster teamwork.

Practicing mindfulness, active listening, and emotional reflection can enhance EI, leading to better personal and professional relationships.

Continuous Learning – Always seeking knowledge, skills, and new experiences to evolve.

Learning is a lifelong journey that never ends. At 71, I am still a student, embracing new knowledge every day. Continuous learning keeps the mind active, opens doors to new opportunities, and enriches life in countless ways. Whether through books, technology, conversations, or personal experiences, the pursuit of knowledge keeps us growing and evolving.

4. **Mindset & Growth** – Adopting a mindset of curiosity, adaptability, and a willingness to learn from failure.

5.   **Balance & Well-being** – Taking care of your mental, emotional, and physical health to sustain long-term progress.

6.   **Contribution & Legacy** – Using your growth to help others and make a meaningful impact in the world.

Steps to Personal Mastery

1.   **Define Your Vision** – What do you want to achieve in life? What does mastery mean to you?

our vision is the foundation of your journey toward success. It provides clarity, direction, and motivation. A well-defined vision helps you stay focused on your goals, make informed decisions, and overcome obstacles.

To define your vision:

Identify Your Passion – What excites and drives you? I am always passionate about my Yoga and Spirituality and my vision is to help millions of people to become healthy , wealthy and spiritually strong

Set Clear Goals – Where do you see yourself in the future?

Visualize Success – Imagine achieving your dreams.

Align with Your Values – Ensure your vision reflects your core beliefs.

Write It Down – A written vision keeps you accountable. In my Journal . I daily write my goals out of which some of them I have already achieved . This is the power of writing your

Goal A strong vision serves as a guiding light, inspiring you to take meaningful action and create the life you desire.

2.   **Identify Your Strengths & Weaknesses** – Self-assessment to know where you need improvement.

Create a Growth Plan – Develop habits and routines that align with your goals.

Seek Mentors & Guidance – Learn from those ahead of you on the path.

Practice Self-Discipline – Stay consistent, even when motivation fades.

Embrace Challenges – View failures as learning opportunities.

Reflect & Adjust – Regularly evaluate your progress and make necessary changes.

The Charioteer and the Path of Mastery

In the great Indian epic, the **Mahabharata**, there is a powerful conversation between Lord Krishna and the warrior prince Arjuna, recorded in the **Bhagavad Gita**. This story provides deep insights into the path of **personal mastery**.

The Dilemma of Arjuna

As Arjuna stands on the battlefield of Kurukshetra, he is overwhelmed with doubt, fear, and confusion. He sees his own relatives, teachers, and loved ones on the opposing side, and his heart fills with sorrow. He drops his bow and refuses to fight, saying,

"My mind is in turmoil. I do not know what is right. Guide me, Krishna!"

Krishna's Teaching: The Chariot as a Metaphor

Krishna, acting as Arjuna's charioteer, does not immediately tell him what to do. Instead, he imparts **timeless wisdom** about self-mastery, duty, and the nature of the self. He compares the human being to a chariot:

- **The chariot itself** represents the body.

- **The horses** symbolize the senses, which are often wild and distracted.

- **The reins** are the mind, which must control the senses.

- **The charioteer (Krishna)** represents wisdom and inner guidance.

- **The passenger (Arjuna)** is the true self, the soul, which must choose the right path.

Krishna teaches Arjuna that **mastery over life begins with mastery over oneself.** If the reins (mind) are loose, the horses (senses) will run wild, leading the chariot astray. But if the charioteer (wisdom) holds the reins firmly, guiding the horses in the right direction, the chariot (life) moves toward its true purpose.

The Lesson: Mastery Through Self-Discipline

Krishna's wisdom teaches us that personal mastery is achieved through:

1.   **Self-Awareness** – Understanding one's inner fears, desires, and emotions.

2.   **Control Over the Mind** – Training the mind to stay focused and disciplined.

3.   **Detachment from Outcome** – Acting with full effort but without being attached to success or failure.

4.   **Devotion and Purpose** – Aligning one's actions with a higher goal or duty (Dharma).

Ultimately, Arjuna finds his strength again and rises as a true warrior—not just on the battlefield, but within himself.

Conclusion

This story reminds us that personal mastery is not about controlling the world but about **controlling ourselves**. Just like Arjuna, we all face doubts and challenges. But by mastering our minds and actions, we can navigate the battlefield of life with confidence, purpose, and inner peace.

Chapter 9: Svar Vigyan And Water Therapy

Svar Vigyan: The Science of Breath and Sound

Svar Vigyan (also spelled Swar Vigyan) is an ancient Vedic science that explores the relationship between breath (Prana) and the cosmic energies governing human life.

It is a branch of yoga and tantra that focuses on the rhythmic patterns of breath (Svaras) and their influence on physical, mental, and spiritual well-being. Rooted in the Tantras and Vedas and known as Swara Yoga

This knowledge is deeply connected to Swara Yoga, which teaches how different breathing patterns (left, right, and balanced nostril breathing) affect our consciousness, energy, and decision-making.

Once, Goddess Parvati asked Lord Shiva, O Lord ! Take mercy on me and reveal to me the knowledge which bestows all prosperity and benefits.

Lord Shiva Repplied This science of Svaras Is a secret of all secrets and reveals the secret of the essence of all benefits. This science is the crest jewel of all knowledge,

In the Shiv Sarvodaya, Lord Shiva imparts deep wisdom to Goddess Parvati on Swar Vigyan (the science of breath).

Swar Vigyan is an ancient yogic science that explains how breathing patterns influence human life, destiny, and spiritual progress.

In yogic and Ayurvedic traditions, **Nadis** are the energy channels through which **prana** (life force) flows in the body. It is believed that there are **72,000 nadis**, though the three most important ones are:

Key Principles of Svar Vigyan

Three Types of Breath Flow (Svaras)

Ida Nadi (Left Nostril - Chandra Svara) → Cooling, lunar energy, linked to the parasympathetic nervous system, enhances intuition and mental clarity.

Pingala Nadi (Right Nostril - Surya Svara) → Heating, solar energy, linked to the sympathetic nervous system, enhances physical activity and digestion.

Sushumna Nadi (Balanced Breath - Shiva Svara) → When both nostrils flow equally, spiritual energy is heightened, making it ideal for meditation and deep awareness.

Timing and Breath Cycles

The dominant nostril changes approximately every 90 minutes in a healthy person.

Understanding when to act based on the active nostril can improve decision-making, health, and success.

Cosmic Influence on Breath

Svar Vigyan also incorporates planetary cycles and lunar influences, determining the best time for activities like business, meditation, or healing.

Relation of Respiration with Age -Ordinarily a human being breathes about 13 to 15 times per minute. Thus, in a full day and night (24 hours) the total number of respirations reaches to about 21000. It is an established fact that lesser is the number of respirations of an organism per minute, the greater is his life-span. In other words, if we control and minimize the number of our respirations, we can increase our life-span.

Benefits of Svar Vigyan

☑ **Physical Health**

Helps in balancing body heat and coolness, preventing diseases.

Enhances metabolism, digestion, and circulation.

Strengthens the immune and nervous system.

☑ **Mental Clarity & Emotional Stability**

Enhances focus, creativity, and decision-making.

Reduces stress, anxiety, and emotional imbalances.

☑ **Spiritual Awakening**

Awakens Kundalini's energy when practiced deeply.

Leads to higher states of consciousness and inner peace.

☑ Improved Timing for Actions

Helps choose the right time for work, meditation, travel, and other important tasks for better outcomes.

Practical Applications of Svar Vigyan

For Energy & Focus → Breathe through the right nostril (Pingala) to activate heat and alertness.

For Calmness & Relaxation, → Breathe through the left nostril (Ida) to activate coolness and relaxation.

For Balance & Meditation → Practice alternate nostril breathing (Nadi Shodhana) to harmonize the energies.

Key Teachings of Lord Shiva on Swar Vigyan in Shiv Sarvodaya:

The Three Types of Swar (Breath Cycles):

Ida Nadi (Left Nostril - Chandra Swar): Associated with coolness, lunar energy, intuition, and mental faculties. Best for activities requiring peace, study, and healing.

Pingala Nadi (Right Nostril - Surya Swar): Represents heat, solar energy, physical activity, and vitality. Ideal for action-oriented tasks and material pursuits.

Sushumna Nadi (Central Channel): When both nostrils flow equally, it leads to spiritual awakening, higher consciousness, and deep meditation.

Understanding the Timing of Swar:

Lord Shiva explains that breath alternates between the left and right nostrils in cycles, and knowing which Swar is active at a given time helps one determine the best course of action.

Using Swar Vigyan for Success:

Starting any important work during the appropriate Swar increases the chances of success.

Left Swar (Chandra) is best for mental work, love, and creativity.

Right Swar (Surya) is favorable for physical activities, war, debates, and leadership. Students who are solving complex problems

Spiritual Awakening through Swar Control:

When the breath flows evenly through both nostrils (Sushumna), it is the best time for meditation and divine connection.

Mastering breath control leads to self-realization and liberation (Moksha).

Health and Longevity:

Monitoring one's Swar can prevent diseases.

Breathing exercises (Pranayama) can purify the body and mind.

Breathing from the wrong nostril at the wrong time can cause imbalances and illness.

Conclusion:

Lord Shiva, in Shiv Sarvodaya, reveals that Swar Vigyan is not just about breathing but a powerful science that governs health, success, and spiritual enlightenment. By understanding the rhythm of our breath, one can harmonize with cosmic energy and attain supreme wisdom.

Swar Vigyan (or Swar Yoga) is an ancient Vedic science that studies the breath and its connection to health and energy. For cancer patients, breathwork and energy-balancing practices can be highly beneficial for reducing stress, improving oxygenation, and supporting overall well-being.

Best Swar Vigyan Practices for Cancer Patients:

Chandra Swar (Left Nostril Breathing - Ida Nadi Activation)

Why? Activates the parasympathetic nervous system, promotes relaxation, and cools the body, which can help counteract inflammation and stress.

How? Close the right nostril and breathe deeply through the left nostril for 5-10 minutes.

Sukh Purvak Pranayama (Gentle Rhythmic Breathing)

Why? Helps reduce anxiety, enhances lung function, and calms the nervous system.

How? Inhale deeply for 4 seconds, hold for 4 seconds, exhale for 6-8 seconds, and repeat.

Nadi Shodhan (Alternate Nostril Breathing)

Why? Balances energy channels (Ida & Pingala), reduces stress and harmonizes bodily functions.

How? Inhale through the left nostril, exhale through the right; then inhale through the right and exhale through the left. Continue for 5-10 minutes.

Ujjayi Pranayama (Ocean Breath or Victorious Breath)

Why? Strengthens the immune system, oxygenates the blood, and soothes the mind.

How? Inhale deeply through the nose while slightly constricting the throat, producing a whispering sound. Exhale in the same manner.

Bhramari Pranayama (Humming Bee Breath)

Why? Reduces pain, calms the nervous system, and enhances mental clarity.

How? Inhale deeply, then hum like a bee while exhaling, feeling the vibrations in the head and throat.

Additional Considerations:

Cancer patients should avoid excessive Surya Swar (right nostril) activation as it increases heat, which may not be suitable for all conditions.

Always practice under expert guidance, especially if undergoing chemotherapy or radiation therapy.

Combining breathwork with meditation, visualization, and gentle yoga can enhance benefits.

Spiritual Water Therapy –

The practice of energizing water with prayers, mantras, or positive affirmations to influence its structure and healing properties.

Does Mantra Influence Water Therapy?

Yes, many spiritual traditions believe that sound vibrations from mantras can influence the molecular structure of water and enhance its healing properties. Some key concepts include:

The Healing Power of Water: A Legacy of Spiritual Therapy

The year was 1967. I was just a child when I first heard the story—one that had been whispered in our family for generations. It was the tale of my father and the panther.

Curiosity consumed me. How could such an incident have happened? One day, unable to hold back my questions any longer, I approached my aunt—my father's sister—and asked her to recount the event. She sighed, her eyes distant, as if reliving a memory from long ago.

"When your father was around fifteen," she began, "he would wake up early every summer morning to collect ripe mangoes that had fallen from the tree. The tree stood not far from our house, and the golden fruit it bore was always worth the effort. But that morning was different. As he reached under the tree, his hands searching in the dark, he unknowingly placed his palm on something warm and alive."

She paused, letting the suspense settle in my young mind. Then, in a hushed voice, she continued.

"It was a tiger."

A shiver ran down my spine.

"In a flash, the beast lunged at him. He screamed, but his voice was swallowed by the stillness of dawn. His body bore deep gashes, and blood pooled around him. He lay there, helpless, his life slipping away. By sheer fate, a passing servant heard a faint, strained breath from the grove. She rushed toward the sound and was met with darkness—and the unmistakable scent of iron in the air. When she spotted the blood, she cried out for help. The villagers gathered, wrapped your father in a bedsheet, and carried him home. Many thought he wouldn't make it."

I hung onto every word, my heart pounding, unable to believe that my father had come so close to death.

Then my aunt's voice softened. "But our great-grandfather was a healer," she said. "He had mastered the art of Spiritual Water Therapy—a sacred practice where water was infused with prayers and mantras to harness its healing power."

With unwavering faith, my great-grandfather began his water healing ritual. He chanted ancient mantras, his voice steady, filling the room with an energy unlike anything else. For an hour, he continued the practice, blessing the water with sacred vibrations. Then, he gently poured it over your father's wounds, washing away the blood clots.

The nearest doctor was miles away, and your father lay unconscious. Some relatives insisted he be taken to the hospital, fearing the worst.

But my great-grandfather, with the conviction of a man who had witnessed miracles, reassured them. "He will live," he said. "The water will heal him."

And it did.

No antibiotics, no medical intervention—only the continuous application of mantra-infused water, poured over his wounds at intervals throughout the day. With each drop, his body responded, his wounds slowly closing, his strength returning.

It wasn't the first time this healing had worked. In our village, my great-grandfather was known far and wide. Those suffering from snake bites, deep wounds, and even mysterious ailments came to him, seeking his sacred water therapy. And time after time, they left healed.

I, too, had experienced this magic. As a child, I had suffered from chicken pox, and while I barely remember the pain, I do remember the ritual. The chanted water was poured over my skin, again and again. And just like my father, I healed.

Looking back, I often wonder—was it the water itself, or the power of intention behind it? Science tells us that water carries memory, that it responds to vibration. And perhaps, just perhaps, when combined with sacred mantras, it becomes something greater—a conduit for healing, a vessel for the universal energy that connects us all.

Spiritual Water Therapy is not just an ancient tradition. It is a testament to the power of faith, vibration, and the unseen forces that shape our existence.

Even today, as modern medicine advances, I believe there are mysteries in nature that remain unexplained—secrets passed down from generations of healers who understood the sacred connection between water, sound, and the human spirit.

Scientific Perspective – Dr. Masaru Emoto's experiments suggest that words, sounds, and intentions can alter the crystalline structure of water, making it more harmonious or chaotic.

Vedic & Yogic Traditions – Mantras like Om, Gayatri Mantra, or Mahamrityunjaya Mantra are believed to purify water, infuse it with positive energy, and promote healing.

Religious Practices – Many faiths use prayers or blessings to sanctify water, such as holy water in Christianity or energized water in Hindu rituals.

How to Practice Mantra-Infused Water Therapy

Take a clean glass or copper vessel filled with water.

Chant a mantra (e.g., Om Namah Shivaya or Gayatri Mantra) while holding the water with a positive intention.

After chanting, drink the water slowly with mindfulness.

Repeat daily to experience potential benefits.

Chapter 10: The Path Within: My Yoga and Spiritual Journey

For decades, I have been a dedicated Yoga and Spiritual Trainer, guiding individuals on a transformative journey toward physical well-being, mental clarity, and inner peace. Yoga has been my passion since childhood, shaping my life and carrying me forward on a profound path of self-discovery and service.

With a deep understanding of ancient yogic practices, Prāṇāyāma, and meditation techniques, I help my students attain harmony in śarīra (body), manaḥ (mind), and ātmā (soul). My approach extends beyond physical āsanas—it embraces the wisdom of adhyātma jñāna (spiritual knowledge), svādhyāya (self-awareness), and prāṇa śakti samatā (energy alignment).

Through personalized sessions, I empower individuals to cultivate mindfulness, reduce stress, and embrace a holistic lifestyle. Whether a beginner or an experienced sādhaka, my goal is to inspire a life of balance, fulfillment, and spiritual awakening through the profound teachings of Yoga and Adhyātma.

Seeking the Roots of Ancient Wisdom

For over three decades, I have been practicing and teaching yoga, continuously deepening my knowledge and refining my techniques. My journey includes:

• Advanced Training in Yoga & Meditation – Completed the Yoga and Advanced Meditation Course from Sidhi Samadhi Yoga (SSY) Headquarters, Mysore, in 1993.

• Spiritual Studies & Sadhana – Member of the Spiritual Science Research Foundation (SSRF), Goa, where I have practiced and undertaken various spiritual sadhanas under the guidance of renowned gurus.

• Vedanta & Scriptural Knowledge – Affiliated with the Chinmaya International Foundation, Kerala, where I pursued online courses in Basic Vedanta, Sanskrit, and Panchadashi, delving deeper into the philosophical roots of yoga and spirituality. I have also attended several seminars organized by CIF.

• Certified Yoga Trainer – Recognized by AYUSH, Government of India, and actively conducting both online and offline yoga and spirituality classes under the banner of Amar Yoga, helping and guiding numerous students on their paths.

• Swami Chidananda World Peace Foundation, Mangalore – Serving as a General Secretary of this esteemed foundation, which upholds the teachings of Swami Chidananda Saraswati, promoting global harmony, selfless service, and spiritual enlightenment.

Through my years of practice and teaching, I have witnessed firsthand the profound impact of yoga and spirituality on the human mind and body. My mission remains unwavering—to share this ancient wisdom, uplift lives, and help others unlock their fullest potential through the power of yoga and inner awareness.

Searching for a Life

The weight of unfulfilled dreams often leads us down unexpected paths. My journey began with a single thought—an unshakable desire to carve a life of my own. The realization struck after I failed my Pre-University exams. The failure wasn't just a mark on paper; it was a turning point, a quiet whisper in my mind urging me to leave home and seek my destiny elsewhere.

Mumbai. The city of dreams, the city of endless possibilities. The thought of moving there took root, refusing to let go. At that time, I was no longer a child, yet not quite an adult. I knew right from wrong, yet life's greatest lessons still lay ahead. Sometimes, we lack the courage to express our deepest desires, fearing rejection or judgment. But I knew one thing—if I didn't take this step, I would never know where life could lead me.

Telling my parents wasn't easy. My mother was strict, yet her love for us knew no bounds. At first, they resisted, unwilling to let me go. But persistence has a way of bending even the firmest resistance. Within a week, my decision was final. I was leaving.

Saying goodbye was the hardest part. My mother, strong and composed, walked behind me to the bus stop, silently wiping away her tears. As the bus roared to life, carrying me toward the unknown, I made a silent vow—I would not return home until I had completed my graduation.

A City of Struggles

Mumbai welcomed me not with open arms, but with the harsh reality of survival. I spent the first few days at my cousin sister's house before my brother took me to work in a relative's hotel. Life in the hotel was grueling—long hours, little rest, and an unfamiliar world filled with endless toil.

After six months, my relative, the hotel owner, informed me that I had to leave. But fate had other plans. Another distant relative agreed to employ me in his hotel, but I had one condition—I wanted to continue my education. I requested time for college, and to my relief, he agreed.

In 1973, I enrolled in college. My days began before dawn—waking up at 4 AM, rushing to college by 6 AM, and then working long shifts at the hotel. Sleep became a luxury, and exhaustion a constant companion. But I endured. Because this was my choice. Because this was my dream.

Five years passed in the blink of an eye, with one lost year due to unforeseen circumstances. Finally, in 1978, I graduated.

In January 1979, I returned home after nearly six years. As I stepped into my house, I saw my mother waiting for me, her eyes brimming with unspoken emotions.

The moment she embraced me, neither of us could hold back our tears. But this time, they were tears of joy.

The Awakening of a Passion

Throughout my struggles, there was always one thing that tugged at my heart—Yoga. It had been a quiet calling, a lingering whisper from childhood. I remembered my father teaching us Śīrṣāsana (Headstand), supporting us with pillows, guiding us gently. The fascination never left me.

One day, while returning home from work, I picked up a yoga book from a railway stall. That book became my first teacher. I began practicing every day, perfecting the āsanas, exploring the breathwork of Prāṇāyāma.

One afternoon, a friend saw me practicing and remarked, "Yoga cannot be learned from books alone. You need a Guru." His words struck me deeply. I knew he was right. The path of Yoga is not just about physical postures—it is a discipline, a spiritual journey. I needed guidance.

At that time, Yoga was not as popular as it is today. Finding a good institute was a challenge. But my search led me to Siddha Samādhi Yoga (SSY), headquartered in Mysore. Though I took the course in Mangalore, it was a turning point in my life. The Advanced Meditation Course opened doors to a world I had never known before.

And from there, my true journey began.

My Dinacharya: A Sacred Start to the Day

The world is still wrapped in silence when I wake at 5 AM. Darkness gently retreats, and a new day unfolds—pure, untouched. This is my sacred hour, my time of alignment.

I rise and stand before the mirror, my own reflection staring back at me. With both palms open, I recite my first prayer:

"Karāgre vasate Lakṣhmīḥ, karamadhye Sarasvatī |

Karamūle tu Govindaḥ, prabhāte karadarśanam ||"

The touch of my palms holds the divine—Lakṣhmī at my fingertips, Sarasvatī in my palms, and Govinda at the base. Wealth, wisdom, and strength—what more does one need to begin the day?

A Tribute to the Divine Feminine

Before stepping forward, I invoke the grace of five legendary women—symbols of resilience, wisdom, and purity. Their stories are woven into the fabric of time, and their remembrance purifies the soul.

"Āhalyā Draupadī Sītā, Tārā Mandodarī tathā |

Pañcakanyā smarennityaṁ mahāpātakanāśinīḥ ||"

These names whisper through the morning air—Ahalya, who rose from a curse; Draupadi, the unwavering; Sita, the embodiment of virtue; Tara, wise beyond ages; Mandodari, the queen of quiet strength.

Their virtues become my armor for the day.

The First Step with Humility

Before my feet touch the ground, I pause. The earth, vast and nurturing, has held my weight every single day. Today, I acknowledge her.

"Samudra Vasane Devi, Parvatastana Mandite |

*Vishnu Patni Namastubhyam, Padasparsham
Kshamasva Me ||"*

I whisper my apology, seeking forgiveness from Bhūmi Devi for the touch of my feet upon her sacred body. The mountains are her bosom, the oceans her flowing garment, and yet, she bears us all.

This moment of humility reminds me—to walk this earth lightly, with reverence.

A Conversation with the Universe

Looking at my reflection once more, I affirm:

"I am the best. I love myself. Creativity flows through me. I give my best to this world. Thank you, Universe, for this beautiful day."

The words settle into my being, not just as thoughts, but as truths waiting to unfold.

Embracing the Morning Light

A splash of cool water awakens my skin, and I step onto the balcony, where the world is still stretching into wakefulness. The breeze carries whispers of dawn, and the sky begins to soften with golden hues.

Facing the east, I close my eyes and offer my gratitude to Surya—the giver of light, energy, and abundance. With each breath, I invoke his twelve sacred names, welcoming his radiance into my soul.

The warmth of the first sunrays touches my face, and in that moment, I am not just a man standing on a balcony.

I am part of something vast, eternal, divine.

Day in Harmony: The Ayurvedic & Yogic Way of Life

As the first golden rays of the Sun kiss the earth, I begin my day with devotion and discipline. My mornings are sacred, infused with the wisdom of Ayurveda and the timeless practices of Yoga. Each moment is a ritual, a step towards aligning my body, mind, and soul with the cosmic rhythm.

Greeting the Sun with Surya Namaskar

The dawn breaks, and I stand in reverence, facing the east, embracing the warmth of the sun. My practice of Surya Namaskar (Sun Salutation) is not merely an exercise but a spiritual offering, each posture resonating with the twelve names of the Sun God:

Om Mitrāya Namaha – Salutations to the friend of all.

Om Ravaye Namaha – Salutations to the shining one.

Om Sūryāya Namaha – Salutations to the one who induces activity.

Om Bhānave Namaha – Salutations to the one who illuminates.

Om Khagāya Namaha – Salutations to the one who moves through the sky.

Om Pushne Namaha – Salutations to the giver of strength and nourishment.

Om Hiraṇyagarbhāya Namaha – Salutations to the golden cosmic self.

Om Marīchaye Namaha – Salutations to the lord of dawn.

Om Ādityāya Namaha – Salutations to the son of Aditi, the cosmic mother.

Om Savitre Namaha – Salutations to the source of all life.

Om Arkāya Namaha – Salutations to the one worthy of praise and glory.

Om Bhāskarāya Namaha – Salutations to the one who radiates divine light.

Purifying the Entrance and Awakening the Body

The entrance to my home is a sacred space, and each morning, I step outside, spill water before my door, and wipe it clean—an age-old ritual inviting positivity and prosperity.

Before brushing my teeth, I practice Usha Paan, a revered Ayurvedic practice, by drinking one glass of lukewarm water followed by two glasses of alkaline water.

This simple yet powerful habit aids in proper evacuation of bowels and bladder, cleansing the system for the day ahead.

Preparation of Alkaline Water:

In the stillness of the night, I prepare a glass jar filled with water, adding slices of lemon, cucumber, fresh pudina (mint) leaves, tulsi (holy basil), and a piece of ginger. By morning, this elixir is charged with nature's healing energy.

Benefits of Alkaline Water:

- Enhances hydration and absorption.

- Balances pH levels, reducing acidity.

- Boosts metabolism and aids digestion.

- Flushes toxins, promoting detoxification.

- Improves energy levels and supports skin health.

- Helps neutralize stomach acid, preventing acid reflux.

The Purification Ritual

With a cleansed body and mind, I proceed to my morning ablutions. Bathing is a sacred act, and on Sundays, I indulge in an oil bath—a rejuvenating ritual that nourishes the body and calms the nervous system.

Guiding the Breath, Nourishing the Body

At 7 AM, I begin my yoga sessions—online or in-person, depending on my students' needs. By 9 AM, it's time for my first meal, a divine offering to my body:

Fruits: Papaya and banana are staples, complemented by seasonal fruits.

Nuts: Almonds, figs (anjir), raisins, and walnuts—soaked overnight for optimal absorption.

Juice and light breakfast.

A brief scan of the newspaper to stay informed.

Post-breakfast, I engage in journal writing, a practice that cultivates self-awareness and mindfulness. As I guide my foreign yoga students through their sessions in the afternoon and evening, my day flows seamlessly between teaching, personal practice, and social commitments.

Nourishment & Movement

Lunch:

A simple yet wholesome meal:

Fresh salad

Two roti (Indian bread)

A bowl of rice

Seasonal vegetables

Evening Walk & Spiritual Practices

As the sun begins its descent, I dedicate 45-60 minutes to an evening walk, absorbing wisdom through inspirational music or spiritual discourses. A refreshing bath follows, culminating in pooja and the recitation of Vishnu

Sahasranama—a practice that brings deep peace and alignment.

Dinner & Wind Down

By 7:30 PM, I have my final meal, similar to lunch but lighter. I avoid excessive television, reserving screen time for insightful content. My online meetings are usually scheduled at night, ensuring a productive end to the day.

Before retiring to bed at 10:30 PM, I follow a simple yet potent nighttime routine:

Wash my feet and brush my teeth.

Massage my toes with oil to stimulate energy points.

Practice Bhramari Pranayama, a humming breath technique that soothes the nervous system, inviting restful sleep.

Ancient Wisdom for Modern Living

The teachings of Maharshi Vagbhata illuminate my path:

The Science of Saliva (Lārā) in Healing:

Morning saliva heals wounds, especially for diabetics.

Treats dark circles and conjunctivitis.

Animals instinctively use saliva for wound healing.

Sleeping Postures & Directions:

Head to the East: Enhances knowledge and enlightenment.

Head to the South: Best for health and prosperity.

Avoid North: Associated with stagnation and disease.

Understanding Ayurveda & Food Choices:

Vata-dominant (75%), Pitta (15%), Kapha (10%)—knowing your constitution is key.

South Indians should consume more rice than wheat.

Running isn't ideal in India due to joint wear and tear; walking is superior.

Europe & USA: Cold-dominant; need high-intensity activities.

The Freedom of the Body:

Natural urges should never be suppressed—sneezing, thirst, yawning, or laughter.

Drinking water at the wrong time can cause ailments:

Post-meal water is poison (Bhojanānte viṣam vāri)—it weakens digestion.

Drink only as per thirst.

Ayurvedic Food Combinations:

Avoid: Milk with jaggery, onion with milk, urad dal with curd, honey with ghee.

Good: Jaggery with ghee.

Eating & Resting Postures:

Sukhasana (cross-legged) enhances digestion; standing destroys it.

Post-meal rest:

Morning/Afternoon: Lie on the left side to activate Pingala Nadi (Solar Energy Channel), aiding digestion.

Evening: Avoid lying down immediately; wait at least two hours.

Vajrasana is the only asana allowed after meals.

Each day unfolds in harmony with nature's rhythms, merging the wisdom of Ayurveda with the discipline of Yoga. By embracing these ancient principles, I experience a life of vitality, balance, and bliss—a journey where body, mind, and spirit dance in perfect synchrony with the universe.

Understanding Yoga and Its Importance in Daily Life

What is Yoga?

Yoga is an ancient practice that originated in India over 5,000 years ago. It is a holistic discipline that integrates physical postures (asanas), breathing techniques (pranayama), and meditation (dhyana) to enhance overall well-being.

The word Yoga is derived from the Sanskrit term Yuj, meaning "to unite" or "to join," symbolizing the harmony of body, mind, and spirit.

Why is Yoga Essential in Daily Life?

In today's fast-paced world, stress, anxiety, and health issues have become prevalent. Incorporating yoga into our daily routine can bring profound benefits across multiple dimensions—physical, vital, mental, emotional, psychic, and spiritual.

Many yogic traditions trace their lineage to Maharshi Patanjali's Yoga Sutras, which define the structured path of yoga through the Eight Limbs of Yoga:

Yama – Cultivating self-discipline and ethical conduct.

Niyama – Developing positive habits and inner purity.

Asana – Practicing postures to prepare the body for meditation.

Pranayama – Controlling breath to regulate life energy.

Pratyahara – Withdrawing the senses from distractions.

Dharana – Focusing the mind for deep contemplation.

Dhyana – Achieving uninterrupted meditation.

Samadhi – Attaining complete absorption and self-realization.

When practiced sincerely and consistently, yoga fosters a healthy, stress-free, and balanced life, leading one toward self-discovery and inner peace.

The Core Philosophy of Yoga

The essence of yoga is beautifully captured in the Sanskrit verse:

"योगश्चित्तवृत्तिनिरोधः" (Yogaś citta-vṛtti-nirodhaḥ)

Yoga (योगः) – Union, discipline, or the practice of yoga.

Citta (चित्त) – Mind or consciousness.

Vṛtti (वृत्ति) – Fluctuations or modifications of the mind.

Nirodhaḥ (निरोधः) – Control or stilling of thoughts.

This sutra defines yoga as "the cessation of the fluctuations of the mind." When the mind attains stillness, free from distractions, true yoga is realized—leading to self-awareness and tranquility.

My Yoga, Pranayama, and Meditation Session

1. Beginning the Practice: Centering the Mind

Seated in Vajrasana – The practice begins in a comfortable and steady posture.

OM Chanting (3–5 times) – To create a positive vibration and calm the mind.

Guru Vandana (Prayer to the Guru) – Offering gratitude to the spiritual teacher:

Gurur Brahma, Gurur Vishnu, Gurur Devo Maheshwaraha...

"The Guru is the Creator (Brahma), the Sustainer (Vishnu), and the Destroyer (Shiva). The Guru is the Supreme Divine, and I bow to that revered Guru."

Additionally, the traditional Patanjali Mangala Shloka is recited to honor Maharshi Patanjali:

Yogena Chittasya Padena Vacham, Malam Sharirasya Cha Vaidyakena...

2. Pranayama: Breath Control Techniques (Seated in Vajrasana)

Abdominal, Thoracic, and Clavicular Breathing – Enhancing breath awareness.

Mudra Practice – Using Chin, Chinmaya, Adi, Merudanda, and Purna Mudras.

Kapalabhati (Cleansing Breath) – Performed in two variations.

Bhastrika Pranayama – Energizing breath (15–20 strokes).

Anulom Vilom (Nadi Shodhana) – Alternate nostril breathing for balance.

Brahmari Pranayama – Performed in two variations, creating a humming vibration.

Advanced Pranayama with Bandhas – Engaging Mula Bandha, Uddiyana Bandha, and Jalandhara Bandha to enhance energy flow.

3. Kriya Yoga & Micro Exercises

Tongue Twisting Kriya Yoga – Performed in three variations, concluding with Shankha Mudra.

Micro Exercises – Performed in a standing position:

Neck Movements (Front-Back, Left-Right, Shoulder Gazing, Full Rotations).

Shoulder & Waist Exercises – To improve flexibility.

Knee and Toe Movements – To strengthen joints and improve mobility.

4. Macro Exercises & Strengthening Postures

Sarvanga Pushti (Full-Body Strengthening).

Hrid Gati (Engine Dhoud).

Anthar Pushti Yoga (Brain Activation).

5. Asana Practice: Postures for Strength & Balance

Surya Namaskar (Sun Salutation) – 12 poses, repeated for 10 rounds.

Standing Asanas:

Ardha Kati Chakrasana – Side bending posture.

Tadasana – Mountain Pose for spinal alignment.

Vrikshasana – Tree Pose for balance.

Trikonasana – Triangle Pose for flexibility.

Seated & Supine Asanas:

Paschimottasana, Bhadrasana, Ardha Matsyendrasana – Forward bends and spinal twists.

Shavasana – Deep relaxation pose.

Pawanmuktasana – Wind-relieving pose.

Advanced Postures:

Shirshasana (Headstand) – The King of Asanas, practiced under expert guidance.

6. Yoga Nidra: The Art of Yogic Sleep (Guided Relaxation – 10 minutes)

Procedure:

Preparation: Lie in Shavasana, palms facing upward, and close your eyes.

Sankalpa (Intention Setting): Mentally repeat a positive affirmation like "I am peaceful and healthy."

Body Scan: Bring awareness to different body parts, releasing tension.

Breath Awareness: Observe the natural rhythm of your breath to calm the nervous system.

Visualization & Sensory Awareness: Experience guided imagery, enhancing deep relaxation.

Returning to Awareness: Gently move fingers and toes, open your eyes, and take a moment before rising.

The Transformative Power of Yoga

Regular yoga practice brings harmony between the body, breath, and mind, fostering physical vitality, emotional balance, and spiritual awakening. As Maharshi Patanjali's teachings suggest, when the fluctuations of the mind are stilled, we experience our true self—a state of profound peace and self-realization.

By integrating yoga into daily life, we embark on a journey not just of fitness, but of inner transformation.

The Power of Yoga Nidra

Deep Relaxation & Stress Reduction – "As you breathe, your body activates the parasympathetic nervous system, melting away stress and anxiety."

Improved Sleep & Relief from Insomnia – "This state mimics deep sleep, healing your mind and body."

Enhanced Concentration & Memory – "By entering the subconscious mind, your focus sharpens effortlessly."

Emotional Healing – "Memories and emotions arise, but instead of suppressing them, you observe and release them."

Creativity & Intuition Awakens – "In stillness, your mind expands beyond boundaries."

Nervous System Balance – "Your heartbeat slows, cortisol drops, and your entire being finds equilibrium."

Physical Healing – "Energy flows freely, strengthening the immune system and soothing pain."

Meditation (15-20 Minutes)

The process and benefits of meditation have already been detailed in an earlier chapter. This practice enhances self-awareness, inner peace, and emotional balance.

Concluding the Practice with a Prayer

सर्वे भवन्तु सुखिनः।

सर्वे सन्तु निरामयाः।

सर्वे भद्राणि पश्यन्तु।

मा कश्चिद् दुःखभाग्भवेत्॥

Sarve bhavantu sukhinaḥ

Sarve santu nirāmayāḥ

Sarve bhadrāṇi paśyantu

Mā kaścid duḥkha-bhāg bhavet

This universal prayer invokes well-being, peace, and happiness for all beings. It embodies the essence of Vasudhaiva Kutumbakam (the world is one family), fostering a spirit of harmony and compassion.

"Yoga Nidra is a gateway to deep rest and rejuvenation. Practice it daily, and you will notice a profound shift."

The Breath of Life: A Lesson in Pranayama

Now that your mind has experienced stillness, let us refine your breath."

Phases of Yogic Breathing (Pranayama)

"Pranayama is the science of breath control. It consists of three fundamental stages—Puraka (inhalation), Kumbhaka (retention), and Rechaka (exhalation). They play a vital role in regulating prana (vital life force) and enhancing overall well-being

1. Puraka (Inhalation) – Drawing in Life Force

Puraka (Inhalation)

Meaning:

The term Puraka refers to the act of inhaling, drawing in fresh air (prana) into the lungs.

Procedure:

Sit comfortably in a meditative posture (such as Padmasana or Sukhasana).

Keep the spine erect and the body relaxed.

Inhale slowly and deeply through the nose.

Expand the chest and abdomen, filling the lungs completely.

Ensure the inhalation is smooth and controlled, avoiding any force.

Purpose:

Introduces fresh oxygen into the body.

Enhances lung capacity and breath awareness.

Prepares the mind and body for deeper states of meditation.

2. Kumbhaka (Retention) – Harnessing Energy

Meaning:

Kumbhaka is the retention of breath, either after inhalation (Antar Kumbhaka) or before exhalation (Bahya Kumbhaka). This phase controls and directs prana within the body.

Procedure:

After inhaling deeply (Puraka), hold the breath inside (Antar Kumbhaka).

Maintain a gentle awareness of the breath, avoiding any strain.

Alternatively, after fully exhaling (Rechaka), retain the breath outside (Bahya Kumbhaka).

The duration of retention varies based on the practitioner's experience.

Mental focus or mantra chanting can be incorporated during this phase.

Purpose:

Improves concentration and enhances mental clarity.

Regulates the nervous system and increases lung efficiency.

Facilitates prana control, deepening meditation.

3. Rechaka (Exhalation) – Letting Go

Meaning:

Rechaka refers to the controlled release of breath, expelling toxins and stagnant air from the lungs.

Procedure:

Slowly and steadily exhale through the nose.

Engage the abdominal muscles slightly to ensure complete exhalation.

Exhalation should be longer than inhalation, following a key Pranayama principle.

Maintain awareness of the breath as it flows out.

Purpose:

Eliminates carbon dioxide and detoxifies the body.

Induces relaxation and calms the nervous system.

Aids in deepening Pranayama practices and spiritual growth.

Integration into Pranayama Practice

These three phases form the foundation of several Pranayama techniques, including:

Nadi Shodhana Pranayama (Alternate Nostril Breathing)

Bhramari Pranayama (Humming Bee Breath)

Kapalabhati (Cleansing Breath)

Anulom Vilom (Controlled Breathing)

For advanced practitioners, a commonly followed breathing ratio is 1:4:2 (Puraka:Kumbhaka:Rechaka). For instance, an inhalation of 4 seconds is followed by breath retention for 16 seconds and an exhalation lasting 8 seconds.

However, beginners should initially focus on smooth, natural breathing without prolonged retention. As they develop proficiency, they can gradually increase the duration of Kumbhaka, enhancing breath control and energy regulation.

The true transformation lies not in changing the external world but in mastering the mind, breath, and inner self. Yoga Nidra and Pranayama are not just practices; they are the keys to unlocking the infinite potential within.

Chapter 11: Brain Power

"The mind is not a vessel to be filled, but a fire to be kindled."

— Plutarch 

The human brain is a remarkable organ, serving as the control center for all cognitive, emotional, and physical functions. It possesses immense potential, enabling us to think, learn, create, and adapt to new situations. Brain power refers to the ability of the mind to process information, solve problems, retain memories, and make decisions efficiently.

Enhancing brain power involves a combination of factors, including proper nutrition, regular physical activity, mental stimulation, and adequate rest. Engaging in lifelong learning, practicing mindfulness, and challenging the brain with puzzles and new experiences can significantly improve cognitive abilities. Moreover, maintaining a positive mindset and reducing stress contribute to better mental performance.

Understanding and harnessing brain power is essential for personal and professional growth, as well as for overall well-being. By nurturing the brain, we can unlock greater creativity, productivity, and resilience in our daily lives.

Brain Is Most Complex Organ

- A 100 billion Nerve Cell

- More Connection than Stars

- Information Travels 268 miles per hour

- Brain is 2% of your Body Wieght , but uses 20 to 30 % of your Calories

- Lose an averague of 85000 cells/ day

- Health of the brain either decelerates Innovation or it accelerates it

Hurts Brsin Injuries

- Brain Injuries

- Drugs and Alchohol

- Obesity

- Smoking

- High Blood Pressure

- Diabities

- Sad Diet

- Enviornmental Toxins

- Lack of Exercise

Enhance Brain Health

- Social Connections

- New Learnings

- Great Diet

- Sleep

- Exercise

- Physical Healthy

- Healthy Anxiety

- Meditation

- Gratitude

Deeper Structures Within the Brain

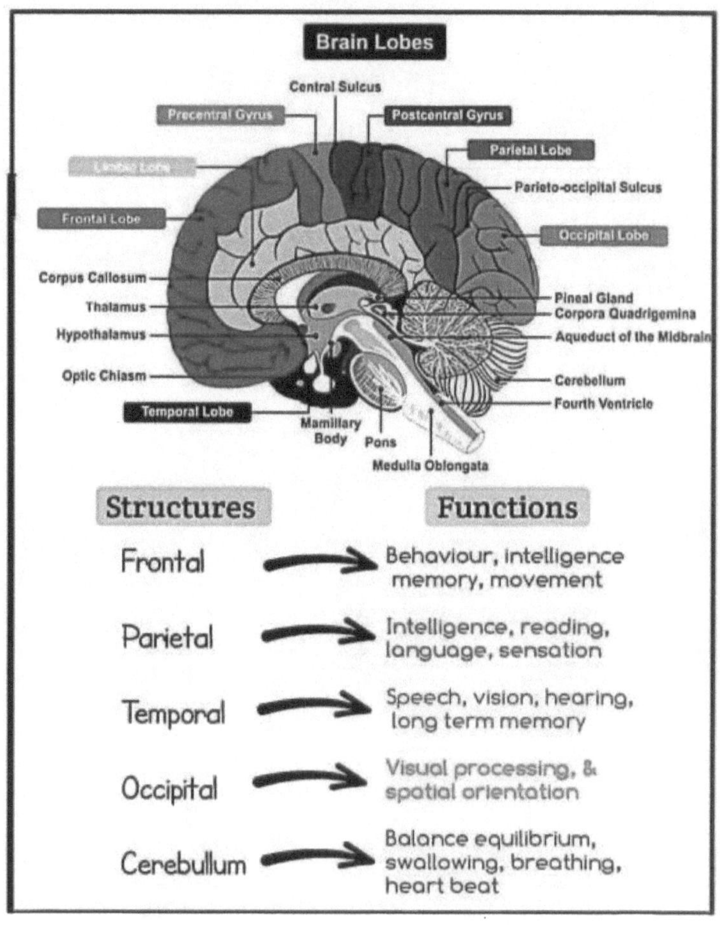

Pituitary Gland

Sometimes called the "master gland," the pituitary gland is a pea-sized structure found deep in the brain behind the bridge of the nose. The pituitary gland governs the function of other glands in the body, regulating the flow of hormones from the thyroid, adrenals, ovaries and testicles. It receives chemical signals from the hypothalamus through its stalk and blood supply.

Hypothalamus

The hypothalamus is located above the pituitary gland and sends it chemical messages that control its function. It regulates body temperature, synchronizes sleep patterns, controls hunger and thirst and also plays a role in some aspects of memory and emotion.

Amygdala

Small, almond-shaped structures, an amygdala is located under each half (hemisphere) of the brain. Included in the limbic system, the amygdalae regulate emotion and memory and are associated with the brain's reward system, stress, and the "fight or flight" response when someone perceives a threat.

Hippocampus

A curved seahorse-shaped organ on the underside of each temporal lobe, the hippocampus is part of a larger structure called the hippocampal formation. It supports memory, learning, navigation and perception of space. It receives information from the cerebral cortex and may play a role in Alzheimer's disease.

Pineal Gland

The pineal gland is located deep in the brain and attached by a stalk to the top of the third ventricle. The pineal gland responds to light and dark and secretes melatonin, which regulates circadian rhythms and the sleep-wake cycle.

Ventricles and Cerebrospinal Fluid

Deep in the brain are four open areas with passageways between them. They also open into the central spinal canal and the area beneath arachnoid layer of the meninges.

The ventricles manufacture **cerebrospinal fluid**, or CSF, a watery fluid that circulates in and around the ventricles and the spinal cord, and between the meninges. CSF surrounds and cushions the spinal cord and brain, washes out waste and impurities, and delivers nutrients.

Blood Supply to the Brain

Two sets of blood vessels supply blood and oxygen to the brain: the **vertebral arteries** and the **carotid arteries.**

The external carotid arteries extend up the sides of your neck, and are where you can feel your pulse when you touch the area with your fingertips. The internal carotid arteries branch into the skull and circulate blood to the front part of the brain.

The vertebral arteries follow the spinal column into the skull, where they join together at the brainstem and form the **basilar artery**, which supplies blood to the rear portions of the brain.

The **circle of Willis**, a loop of blood vessels near the bottom of the brain that connects major arteries, circulates blood from the front of the brain to the back and helps the arterial systems communicate with one another.

Boost Your Brain Power: Tips for a Sharper Mind

Your brain is the control center of your body, influencing everything from decision-making to memory and creativity. Just like a muscle, your brain needs exercise, proper nutrition, and care to function at its best. Here are some powerful ways to enhance your brainpower and stay mentally sharp.

1. Eat Brain-Boosting Foods

Your diet plays a crucial role in brain function. Nutrient-rich foods help improve memory, focus, and overall cognitive ability.

- **Omega-3 Fatty Acids** – Found in fish, walnuts, and flaxseeds, these improve brain function.

- **Dark Chocolate** – Contains flavonoids, caffeine, and antioxidants that boost memory.

- **Berries** – Blueberries, strawberries, and blackberries protect the brain from aging.

- **Nuts & Seeds** – Rich in vitamin E, they help prevent cognitive decline.

2. Stay Physically Active

Exercise isn't just for the body—it benefits the brain too!

- **Aerobic Exercise** – Running, cycling, and swimming increase blood flow to the brain.

- **Yoga & Meditation** – Reduce stress and enhance focus.

- **Strength Training** – Improves memory and mental resilience.

3. Challenge Your Mind

Keeping your brain engaged helps build new neural pathways.

Solve Puzzles – Try crosswords, Sudoku, or chess to enhance problem-solving skills.

Read Regularly – Books, articles, or research papers expand knowledge and critical thinking.

Learn a New Skill – Whether it's a language, instrument, or craft, new skills boost brain flexibility.

4. Get Quality Sleep

Rest is crucial for memory consolidation and problem-solving.

Aim for **7-9 hours of sleep** per night.

Avoid screens **an hour before bedtime** to reduce blue light exposure.

Stick to a **consistent sleep schedule** to optimize brain function.

5. Manage Stress

- Chronic stress can shrink brain size and impact memory.

- Practice **deep breathing, mindfulness, or meditation**.

- Spend time in **nature** for mental relaxation.

- Engage in **laughter and social interactions** to lower stress hormones.

6. Stay Socially Connected

Engaging with others stimulates the brain and prevents mental decline.

- Join social groups, clubs, or volunteer activities.

- Engage in meaningful conversations and debates.

- Keep in touch with friends and family.

7. Hydration & Brain Health

Your brain is 75% water, so staying hydrated is essential for concentration and clarity.

- Drink at least **8 glasses of water daily**.

- Herbal teas and fresh fruit juices also contribute to hydration.

Conclusion

By adopting these habits, you can boost your brainpower and maintain cognitive function for years to come. Small daily changes can lead to big improvements in memory, focus, and overall mental well-being. Start today and give your brain the power it deserve

The Power of the Mind & Wisdom

- **Proverbs 2:6** – *"For the Lord gives wisdom; from His mouth come knowledge and understanding."*

- **Proverbs 4:7** – *"Wisdom is the principal thing; therefore get wisdom: and with all thy getting get understanding."*

- **James 1:5** – *"If any of you lacks wisdom, let him ask of God, who gives to all liberally and without reproach, and it will be given to him."*

Renewing & Strengthening the Mind

- **Romans 12:2** – *"Do not conform to the pattern of this world, but be transformed by the renewing of your mind. Then you will be able to test and approve what God's will is—His good, pleasing and perfect will."*

- **2 Timothy 1:7** – *"For God has not given us a spirit of fear, but of power and of love and of a sound mind."*

Intelligence & Understanding as a Gift from God

- **Daniel 1:17** – *"To these four young men God gave knowledge and understanding of all kinds of literature and* *learning. And Daniel could understand visions and dreams of all kinds."*

- **Exodus 35:31-32** – *"And He has filled him with the Spirit of God, in wisdom, in understanding, in knowledge, and in all manner of workmanship."*

Controlling Thoughts & Thinking Rightly

- **Philippians 4:8** – *"Finally, brethren, whatever things are true, whatever things are noble, whatever things are just, whatever things are pure, whatever things are lovely, whatever things are of good report, if there is any virtue and if there is anything praiseworthy—meditate on these things."*

- **2 Corinthians 10:5** – *"Casting down imaginations, and every high thing that exalteth itself against the knowledge of God, and bringing into captivity every thought to the obedience of Christ."*

Conclusion

The Scipture encourages wisdom, knowledge, and the use of our mind to glorify God. It teaches that intelligence and understanding are gifts from God and should be nurtured with discipline, prayer, and right thinking.

The **Amritabindu Upanishad** is a minor Upanishad belonging to the **Atharvaveda** and is primarily focused on the nature of the **mind** and the **Self (Ātman)**. It teaches that the mind is both the cause of bondage and liberation.

Key Teachings on the Mind

1. **The Mind is Central to Liberation and Bondage**

Mana eva manushyanam

karanam bandhamokshayoh |

bandhaya vishayasaktam

muktam nirvishayam smritam ||"

Meaning:

The **mind** is the key factor that determines whether a person is bound (trapped in suffering) or liberated (free from suffering).

A **mind attached to sensory pleasures** leads to bondage.

A **mind free from worldly attachments** leads to liberation.

This verse emphasizes the importance of controlling and refining the mind to attain spiritual freedom. It aligns with the teachings of Vedanta, which highlight **self-awareness and detachment** as the path to moksha (liberation).

2. **The Pure Mind Reflects the Self**

   o A mind free from distractions and attachments reflects the **Supreme Reality (Brahman)** just as a still lake reflects the sky without distortion.

3. **Beyond the Mind Lies the Ultimate Truth**

- o The Upanishad teaches that **truth is beyond words and thoughts**. To realize Brahman, one must go beyond intellectual reasoning and experience the pure Self directly.

4. **Detachment and Meditation Lead to Liberation**

- o One must withdraw the mind from **external distractions** and focus inward through meditation.

- o This process leads to **Self-realization**, where one sees the unity between the individual self (Jivatman) and the Supreme Self (Paramatman).

Core Verse Example

> *"Yadā manoh nirviṣayaṁ viraktaṁ*
>
> *Tadā paraṁ brahma samāpnuvīta."*

"When the mind becomes detached from sense objects and free from desires, one attains the Supreme Brahman."

Conclusion

The **Amritabindu Upanishad** emphasizes **mental discipline, detachment, and self-inquiry** as the keys to spiritual liberation. It resonates with **Advaita Vedanta** philosophy, teaching that **Brahman alone is real, and the purified mind realizes this truth.**

There will be Peace in the Ultimate Reality Too

There is a mantra in the Rigveda to invoke peace , Iut says " Let there be peace on the land . Let there be peace on the sky. Let there be a peace in water . Let there be peace in Medicines.Let therebe peace in plants . Let there be peace in the entire universe and beyond . Let there be peace in the mulimate reality Let there be peace everywhere.Finally there will peace in me. Om Peace Peace Peace,

Peace implies order. Departure from order is a disturbance. Since nothing is fully in order , we cannot get rid of Altogether. In that case ther degree of disturbance plays an important role. the more the disturbance less peacefull we are. We have a dual nature static and dynamic both acting at the same time. At agiven instant body may be static but the mind is dynamic . In the language of science the mind is itinerant, while the body is localised. The bhagawat Gita says , and we also know , it is difficult to make the mind localised. If wecan control the mind, then we can regulate peace in ourselves. If we are peacefull then we can influence the state of peacefullness around us. If we are powerfull or influential , the range of our control is widespread.

The bhagawad Gita again has a prescription as to how we can be peacefull. Knowledge and self control can lead us to a peacefull mind. When we have an abundance of peace in ourselves, it automatically diffuse the surroundings . Diffusion is a natural process, It flows from abundance to scarcity . Howevr its not a free flow . It can encounter disturbing barriers. If disturbances are minimised then diffusion is smooth .

Self control is the biggest challange to anybody . The biggest impediments in the process of self control are desire Greed and Anger .

The Gita prescribes two kind of human nature devine and demoniac . The degree of self control is more in devine people. A devine person is insensitive to the duality of nature. His reactions are cautious and prudent to the changes. Hovwer demoniac people can be decietfull and egoistic. These people are not a peace, therfore no positivity comes from them . Hovwer there are are instances of complete transforation . It can happen in a positive enviornment.

Its not strange , therefore to see a bright speck and streak of light in a dark cloud. There is a scientific reason . too clouds have water molecules. These molecules interact amomg themselves and, asa result , there is molecular excitation. This process is not unilateral .

War desroys peace . It sometimes makes us feel helpless. It appears as if some sort of destiny controls everything. Perhaps destiny is written by some kind of ultimate reality .

Therefore the Convocation says " let there be peace in the Ultimate realty Too.

MIMD: Mind Your Own Mind – A Cognitive Approach to Mental Well-being

Abstract

The concept of *Mind Your Own Mind* (MIMD) emphasizes cognitive self-awareness, emotional regulation, and mental resilience. This article explores MIMD from a neuropsychological perspective, highlighting its role in stress management, cognitive flexibility, and emotional intelligence.

Introduction

In modern neuroscience, self-directed cognitive regulation is gaining attention. MIMD is a framework for maintaining mental well-being through conscious thought management, mindfulness, and self-reflection. Understanding how the brain processes emotions and thoughts allows individuals to develop healthier coping strategies.

Neurobiological Basis

The prefrontal cortex (PFC) plays a crucial role in cognitive control, while the amygdala regulates emotions. MIMD encourages a balanced interaction between these regions, fostering emotional resilience and reducing anxiety. Mindfulness meditation and cognitive behavioral strategies can enhance neural plasticity, strengthening pathways for emotional regulation.

Clinical Implications

• **Stress Reduction**: MIMD techniques, such as controlled breathing and cognitive reframing, lower cortisol levels and improve stress response.

• **Cognitive Flexibility**: Practicing self-awareness enhances adaptability, reducing rigid thought patterns linked to anxiety and depression.

• **Emotional Intelligence**: Increased self-regulation supports better interpersonal relationships and decision-making.

Conclusion

MIMD is a valuable cognitive approach to maintaining mental health. By cultivating self-awareness and emotional regulation, individuals can foster psychological resilience and improve overall well-being. Future research should explore its application in therapeutic settings for anxiety, depression, and stress-related disorders.

1. A brain freeze is really a sphenopalatine ganglioneuralgia. It happens when something you eat or drink something that's cold. It chills the blood vessels and arteries in the very back of the throat, including the ones that take blood to your brain. These constrict when they're cold and open back up with they're warm again, causing the pain in your forehead.

2. Dreams are believed to be a combination of imagination, phycological factors, and neurological factors.

They prove that your brain is working even when you are sleeping.

3. It is a myth that humans only use 10 percent of our brain. We actually use all of it. We're even using more than 10 percent when we sleep.

4. Over the course of human evolution, brain size has tripled.

5. Your brain uses about the same amount of power as a 15 watt light bulb.

6. Older brains aren't slower because they're weaker, but because they hold more information.

7. Your brain is only about 2% of your body mass, but uses up to 20% of its blood.

8. The brain can survive for up to 6 minutes after the heart stops.

9. Your brain can't feel pain.

10. A human brain can do more computations per second than a powerful supercomputer.

11. If your brain's cortex were laid out flat, it would be about the size of a newspaper page.

Conclusion: The Alchemy of the Mind

Life is an ever-flowing river, sometimes turbulent, sometimes serene. I have walked through the darkest valleys of despair, once standing at the edge where existence itself seemed unbearable. But just as the night surrenders to the dawn, my journey led me from the brink of self-destruction to the vast expanses of self-realization.

The very mind that once shackled me in fear and hopelessness became my greatest ally when I chose to understand it rather than fight it. I discovered that within each of us lies the potential for transformation, for healing, for awakening.

Through yoga and spiritual practice, I learned that the mind is not our enemy—it is a tool, a sacred instrument that, when tuned rightly, plays the divine music of life.

I often wonder: what if I had succumbed to that fleeting moment of despair? What wisdom, what service, what joy would have been lost? But life had a different script for me— one that I had to rewrite with my own awareness, discipline, and surrender.

Now, as a yoga and spiritual master, I share this not as a tale of victory, but as a testimony to the power of the human spirit. If I could emerge from the abyss, so can you.

If I could rewire my mind, so can you. Your mind is your greatest gift—nurture it, guide it, and it will lead you to freedom.

As you close this book, I leave you with this thought: **Your mind does not control you. You are the master. You hold the key. Choose to unlock the highest version of yourself.**

May your journey be filled with light, wisdom, and boundless love.

CONCLUDING PART: A JOURNEY FROM DARKNESS TO LIGHT

As I reflect on my life's journey, I see a path that has taken me from the depths of despair to the highest peaks of inner peace. My childhood was marked by suffering, confusion, and a desperate search for escape.

I remember the painful moments that led me to the brink, my mind clouded by hopelessness, my heart burdened by emotions too heavy for a child to carry. I stood at the edge of existence, believing that there was no way forward.

But life had other plans for me. A spark—small yet powerful—led me toward a path of healing. That path was not easy, nor was it immediate, but it was transformative. Yoga and spirituality became my lifeline, the gentle yet firm hands that pulled me from darkness into light. With each breath, each movement, and each moment of stillness, I discovered a new way to exist—not merely to survive, but to thrive.

Through yoga, I learned that my body was not my enemy but my ally. Through meditation, I understood that my thoughts did not define me; I had the power to observe them without being controlled by them.

Through spirituality, I realized that life is not something that happens to us but something we create with every choice, every action, and every moment of awareness.

My journey has taught me that pain is not the end of the road—it is a passage, a turning point, an opportunity for transformation. What once seemed like an unbearable burden became the foundation upon which I built my resilience, my wisdom, and my peace. The very mind that once tormented me has now become my greatest source of strength.

If there is one message I want to leave with you, it is this: No matter how dark the night, the sun always rises. No matter how lost you feel, there is always a path forward. Your mind is not your enemy—it is your most powerful tool. Learn to nurture it, to understand it, and to guide it. In doing so, you will not only find your way, but you will also illuminate the way for others.

I am here today because I chose to mind my own mind. And now, I invite you to do the same.

With love and light,

Amarnath J Shetty

Disclaimer

The information presented in this book is for informational and educational purposes only. The author and publisher have made every effort to ensure the accuracy and reliability of the content, but they make no representations or warranties regarding the completeness, suitability, or applicability of the information contained herein.

This book is not intended to replace professional advice, whether medical, legal, financial, psychological, or otherwise. Readers are encouraged to consult with qualified professionals for specific concerns or circumstances.

The author and publisher shall not be held liable for any direct or indirect consequences resulting from the application of the information provided in this book. Any reliance on the content is at the reader's own discretion and risk.

The names, characters, and events in any fictional portions of this book are products of the author's imagination. Any resemblance to real persons, living or dead, or actual events is purely coincidental.

A Tribute To My Wife And My In-Laws

Life is a journey filled with relationships that shape us, support us, and leave a lasting impact on our souls. Among those who have profoundly influenced my life, my beloved wife and my in-laws hold a special place. Their love, kindness, and unwavering support have been a source of strength and inspiration to me, and though they are no longer physically present, their memories continue to guide me every day.

My wife was more than just my partner; she was my confidante, my pillar of strength, and my greatest cheerleader. Through every challenge and triumph, she stood by my side, encouraging me with her wisdom and unconditional love. Her presence brought warmth to my life, and her absence has left a void that words cannot fill. Yet, I cherish the beautiful moments we shared, the laughter, the deep conversations, and the countless ways she enriched my life. She taught me the true meaning of love, selflessness, and companionship, and for that, I am eternally grateful.

Equally significant was the love and respect I received from my in-laws. From the very beginning, they welcomed me into their family with open arms, treating me as their own son. Their affection and generosity made me feel not like an outsider, but like a cherished member of their family. They showered me with kindness, wisdom, and support, standing by me in moments of need. Their love was a rare blessing, and I count myself fortunate to have experienced it.

Though my wife and in-laws are no longer with me, their love continues to illuminate my path. I hold onto their memories with a heart full of gratitude, and I strive to honour their legacy by embodying the values they instilled in me. Their love lives on, not just in my heart but in the lessons, they taught me and the person I have become because of them.

This note is not just a remembrance but a heartfelt tribute to the extraordinary souls who blessed my life. Their love was a gift, and their legacy remains an everlasting source of strength and inspiration. I miss them dearly, but I find solace in knowing that love transcends time and space, and in my heart, they will forever remain.

May I Ask You For A Small Favor?

First, I want to thank you for reading this book. You could have chosen any other book, but you took mine, and I appreciate this. I hope you have at least a few actionable insights that will positively impact your daily life.

Can I ask for 30 seconds more of your time?

I'd love it if you could leave a review of the book. That will help me grow my readership by encouraging folks to take a chance on my books.

Keeping it straight - reviews are the lifeblood of any author.

It will take less than a minute of your time but will tremendously help me reach out to more people.

If you liked this book, please consider posting an honest review on your preferred retailer. And I'd love to see your review. Thanks for your support.